# ART DECO
# NEW YORK

For: Pete,

with thanks and
affectionate Regards,

Nov. 17, 2004

# ART DECO
# NEW YORK

DAVID GARRARD LOWE

Watson-Guptill Publications / New York

# ‖ FOR SALLY FORBES ‖

Editor: Sylvia Warren
Senior Production manager: Ellen Greene
Designer: Eric Janssen Strohl, Eric Baker Design Associates

OPPOSITE TITLE PAGE
Paul Manship's *Prometheus*, dedicated in 1934, is Rockefeller Center's best known sculpture. (Photograph by Esther Bubley.)

ISBN: 0-8230-0284-5

First published in 2004 by Watson-Guptill Publications,
a Division of VNU Business Media, Inc.
770 Broadway, New York, N.Y.
www.watsonguptill.com

The publication of *Art Deco New York* was made possible, in part, by a grant from
Furthermore, a program of the J. M. Kaplan Fund.

**Library of Congress Cataloging-in-Publication Data**

Lowe, David.
  Art Deco New York / David Garrard Lowe
    p. cm
  Includes index
  ISBN 0-8230-0284-5
1. Art deco (Architecture)—New York (State)—New York. 2. Architecture—New York (State)—20th Century.
3. New York (N.Y.)—Buildings, structures, etc. I. Title.
  NA735.N5L688    2004
  720'.9747'109041—dc22

                                          200401586

Printed in the United Kingdom
First printing, 2004

1 2 3 4 5 6 7 8 9 / 10 09 08 07 06 05 04

# ACKNOWLEDGMENTS

I must begin my list of those who have helped with this book with John Cadenhead, the superb photographer, one of whose photographs graces the cover of this volume and whose other photographs may be found throughout its pages.

A number of people and institutions were invaluable to my research in New York City.

I would especially like to thank Janet Parks of the Avery Architecture and Fine Arts Library of Columbia University; William Piel, librarian of the New York Society Library; William S. Lieberman of the Metropolitan Museum of Art; Gerard Widdershover and Christopher Knight of Maison Gerard; Christobel Gough of The Society for the Architecture of the City; Richard E. Slavin III, curator of the F. Schumacher & Co. Collection; Scott Bedio, archivist of the Salvation Army; Douglas DiCarlo, archivist of the La Guardia and Wagner Archives; Fritz Harding of the Art Deco Society; the photographers, Dennis Adler and Bo Parker; and the late Gordon McCullom of the American Architectural Archives.

In Chicago, I was given splendid help by Anna Weaver; Edward Morris Bakwin; and by Annemarie van Roessel and Mary Woolever of the Burnham/Ryerson Library of the Art Institute of Chicago.

A particularly rich source of information on the 1920s and 1930s was The Wolfsonian in Miami Beach. Cathy Leff, the director, and Frank Luca assisted me. I would also like to thank the founder of The Wolfsonian, Mitchel T. Wolfson, Jr.

Libraries and archives abroad proved to be superb sources of information and images. In Paris I would like to thank Liza Daum of the Department des Photographies, Bibliothèque Historique de la Ville de Paris; Melle Comminges of the Roger-Viollet Archives; and Thomas Gunther. In Vienna I was aided by Dr. Mattias Boeckl of the Institut fur Architektur, Universitat fur angewandte Kunst Wein. In Montreal I was helped immeasurably by Marie-Chantal Anctil of the Canadian Centre for Architecture.

I am particularly grateful for the information provided to me by experts on a variety of subjects: Kathleen M. Clair and Robert Wallace Blake, both formerly with Pan American World Airways; Delinda Stephens Buie of the University of Louisville; James Reed of the Rockefeller Center Archives and Sandra Manley of The Rockefeller Group; Gene Nocolelli of the Greyhound Bus Museum; and Sam Daniel of the Library of Congress.

No list of acknowledgments for this project would be complete without a mention of those friends and acquaintances who contributed to its completion in many important ways: Joan Davidson, Sheila Chapline, The Reverend Canon Barry E. B. Swain, Mrs. Ely Jacques Kahn, Anne Kaufman Schneider, Molly Rea, Merrideth Miller, Michael Stier, Shelley M. Clark, Mr. and Mrs. John G. Winslow, James W. Guedry, Francis P. King, Hugh A. Dunne, Katherine Brush, Myron Magnet, Marilyn Perry, Christopher Cooley, Patricia Bakwin Selch, Carol Riechers, Addie Sels, and James H. Burke.

Finally, a special thank you is owed to those who were in on the conception of this book and were key to its birth. I would like to mention Sally Forbes, who helped immeasurably with the preparation of the manuscript and with picture research. I would like to note the unfailing interest shown by Sharon Kaplan of Watson-Guptill; and the encouragement of my agent, Noah Lukeman. One last bow must go to my editor, Sylvia Warren, who brought to the project not only her intelligence, but also her extraordinary talent and experience.

They seem as much a part of New York City's physiognomy as the crystalline rock upon which it stands, the tidal Hudson to the west, and the islands scattered in the Upper Bay. So flawlessly do the Chrysler Building, the Empire State, the RCA express and embody New York's urban land-scape that it is virtually impossible to picture the city without them.

When, in the early 1960s, I settled permanently in New York and landed a job with a magazine on Madison Avenue, it was these edifices and others like them constructed in the 1920s and 1930s which reaffirmed to me daily that I dwelt in an incomparable city in which man had raised Everests above neon rainbows. My dentist was located in Rockefeller Center's International Building and every time I passed Lee Lawrie's brawny bronze *Atlas* which adorned the building's small court and entered the luminous spinach-green marble lobby, I was struck anew by how different they were from the barren plazas then being scattered across Manhattan and the new office building lobbies whose gunmetal gray walls proclaimed nothing other than their low maintenance costs.

As a writer, I was intrigued by an epoch, which I had already christened "The Art Deco Era," that could give birth to the Empire State and to Rockefeller Center. Slowly, over time, like the tesserae of a mosaic, the pieces fell into place, until, at last, I had a complete picture. These tesserae came from a multitude of sources. As I began to know and to love the songs of those New York masters of American *lieder*—Cole Porter, Irving Berlin, and others—I perceived a link between them and the architecture of the 1920s and 1930s. The beauty and wit of the Chrysler's pyrotechnic spire was as one with the beauty and wit of a Porter lyric or a Berlin ballad.

And the era came alive for me in the old copies of *Vanity Fair* and *Vogue* with their reportage of high jinks at El Morocco and the smart advertisements for Hattie Carnegie, Bendels, and Peck and Peck which I found in the Manhattan flea markets I haunted. Now and then in a thrift shop there appeared a thrilling artifact of the epoch, an Al Smith for President button, a silk scarf imprinted with the Trylon and Perisphere of the 1939 World's Fair.

That eminent New Yorker, Henry James, observed that the most intriguing historical periods were not those of the distant past, but the past which one could almost reach out and touch. As I moved from one magazine job to another—*Look, American Heritage, McCall's*—the two decades between the First and Second World Wars would, from time to time, miraculously materialize in the people I had the good luck to meet and to befriend: Dorothy Fields, who told me that the best compliment she ever received was when, after she had written the lyrics for "I Won't Dance," Fred Astaire telephoned and announced, "Dorothy, those are the best words I ever danced to" and Anita Loos, who beguiled me with the hilarious story of the attention-getting babe who became Lorelei in *Gentlemen Prefer Blondes*.

One piece that helped complete my image of the Deco decades was very personal. I realized that when I was a small child I had glimpsed the era at its very end, observed, as it were, its last foxtrot just before battle silenced the band. I can date the divide infallibly, for my mother died young, in 1939, so any recollection I have of her must have been from the 1930s. No recollection is more vivid than that of the annual spring journey my father, mother, and I made from Chicago, where we lived, to New York aboard the *Twentieth Century Limited*. Departing the Windy City from the La Salle Street Station, we made our way over an especially laid down red carpet and entered the gleaming silver streamliner. After settling into our drawing room, we headed for the club car, whose tubes of bright light on the ceiling and enormous photomurals at either end, one of Chicago and one of New York, fascinated me. After dinner I would be put to bed and then in the morning, along with breakfast, appeared the broad back of the Hudson, followed by the city itself, its towers offering the same promise of excitement and opportunity to those who arrived by land from the West as did the Statue of Liberty to those who arrived by sea from the East.

As the concept of the volume I wanted to write on the Art Deco era took shape, I realized that it would have to be a book about more than architecture. The German philosopher Friedrich von Schelling wrote that architecture is "music in space . . . frozen music." The music of which the structures of the Deco years were composed consisted not only of stone, steel, and glass, but also of the spirit of the time. Thus I knew that my book would have to include essays on subjects as varied as the experience of American doughboys in France during the Great War, the transformation of society by the appearance of the new woman, and the aesthetic impact on New York of the 1925 Paris exposition. The book would have to be a rich mélange of Coco Chanel and Mayor Jimmy Walker, of Dorothy Parker and designer Donald Deskey, of barkeep Texas Guinan and debutante Brenda Frazier.

The intricate complexity of the era is wonderfully exemplified by an event which took place in the hot late spring of 1939. On the afternoon of June 10, following their day-long tour of the New York World's Fair, King George VI and Queen Elizabeth of England motored north to Hyde Park to spend the weekend with President and Mrs. Franklin D. Roosevelt. The visit to the United States, the first by a reigning British monarch, did much, in the words of *The New York Times*, to create an "era of good feeling" between the two English-speaking nations. That *entente cordiale* would have historic consequences, for within two months Adolph Hitler had unleashed his blitzkrieg against Poland. The second day of "Their Britannic Majesties'" sojourn at Hyde Park, a Sunday, the Roosevelts hosted an afternoon picnic. At that relaxed gathering atop a sunlit hill on the family estate, Mrs. Roosevelt served the visiting royals the historic, the politically astute, the populist hot dog. But there was nothing populist about Mrs. Roosevelt's attire that morning when she and the President, accompanied by the King and Queen, attended church. Then, revealing herself to be a true citizen of the realm of Art Deco, Mrs. R. wore an especially made blue chiffon ankle-length gown, and the First Lady's broad-brimmed silk net "Gainsborough-type" hat came from no less a milliner than Lilly Daché.

— DAVID GARRARD LOWE, NEW YORK

One of Fifth Avenue's first large commercial Art Deco structures was that which Warren & Wetmore designed in 1929 for Stewart & Co. at the southeast corner of Fifth Avenue and 55st Street. Within a year it was occupied by Bonwit Teller, who asked Ely Jacques Kahn to carry out significant remodeling. Bonwits was replaced by the Trump Tower in 1983. (Library of Congress.)

# TABLE OF CONTENTS

OPPOSITE PAGE Nighttime, New York, 1937. Towering over all is the 1,252-foot-tall Empire State Building which opened May 1, 1931. (Library of Congress.)

# PARIS - 1925

# EXPOSITION INTERNATIONALE DES ARTS DÉCORATIFS ET INDUSTRIELS MODERNES

## AVRIL - OCTOBRE

IMPRIMERIE DE VAUGIRARD - PARIS

# INTRODUCTION: IN THE TIME OF ART DECO

There is a splendid symmetry to the era. It commences with the conclusion at Versailles in 1919 of the First World War, the war that was ballyhooed as a "crusade for democracy," and ends with the Nazi invasion of Poland in September of 1939 at the very moment when the New York World's Fair was vigorously promoting the idea that the future would be an epoch of cloudless skies and universal happiness. War and War encloses the decades of the 1920s and 1930s like an iron parentheses. But in those 20 years New York metamorphosed from a grand American metropolis into a world city.

On that dollop of earth lying between the Hudson River and the Atlantic Ocean a new American consciousness was whelped. It was a sensibility composed of elements that could have flourished only in a vast and tolerant city whose high buildings, like the walls of gardens, protect and permit exotic growths to take root and blossom in their shelter. This is why so much of the talent, eccentricity, and genius of the American continent was swept eastward into Gotham's embrace, to meet there immigrants pushed westward across the ocean.

On that stone-hulled ship, that glimmering city, moored just off the East Coast of the United States, Dorothy Parker would write verses unapologetically praising living life on the edge. "On Cheating the Fiddler," published in her 1929 collection *Sunset Gun*, Parker brittlely embraces the philosophy of *carpe diem*:

> *"Then we will have to-night!" we said.*
> *"To-morrow—may we not be dead?"*
> *The morrow touched our eyes; and found*
> *Us walking firm above the ground.*
> *Our pulses quick, our blood alight.*
> *Tomorrow's gone—we'll have tonight!*

In that city Gertrude Vanderbilt Whitney, sculptor and heiress, would found a Museum in Greenwich Village where contemporary American artists—Stuart Davis, Isamu Noguchi, Jo Davidson, among others—could be viewed and whose opening night parties were a far cry from anything seen in Dubuque; in that city sprouted nightclubs where the couplings and uncouplings, the coiffures and catty asides of the denizens were the morning fare of newspaper

ABOVE F. Schumacher & Co.'s cut silk velvet was a magnificent example of highly sophisticated Art Deco design. The person responsible for introducing a modern line at Schumacher was Pierre Pozier, who regularly visited France, the site of the company's textile mills, to view the latest work of artists such as Matisse and Picasso for design ideas. (F. Schumacher & Co.)

OPPOSITE One of the three official posters for the fair which gave Art Deco its name. This one was designed by the brilliant French painter and graphic artist Robert Bonfils. (Private Collection.)

readers from Baltimore to Burbank; in that city Broadway composers like George Gershwin drowned the genteel notes of "Sweet and Low" beneath the emphatic syncopation of "I Got Rhythm." And most curiously, it was this city which was the hometown to that quintessential East Coast aristocrat, Franklin Delano Roosevelt, who, at his inauguration on March 4, 1933, would, in an accent redolent of Groton, Harvard, and Gotham's very best clubs, rally a deeply depressed nation with the galvanic words, "The only thing we have to fear is fear itself." And along the way, as opulent memorials of these packed and teeming decades, New Yorkers would erect fabulous cenotaphs to the age: the Waldorf-Astoria, the Empire State, the Chrysler Building, Rockefeller Center.

Art Deco is a malleable term. It derives from the remarkable design show held in Paris in 1925, the Exposition Internationale des Arts Décoratifs et Industrials Modernes. That exposition was a showcase for the style, not its birthplace, much the way that the World Columbian Exposition held in Chicago in 1893 was a manifestation of the triumph of Beaux Arts architecture, not the place where the style was introduced to Americans. The chairman of the Chicago fair's board of architects, Richard Morris Hunt, had already accomplished that feat by planting rows of Beaux Arts palaces on New York's Fifth Avenue and atop the rocky cliffs of Newport, Rhode Island. Art Deco's genesis was in those seminal years between 1900 and 1914 when the foundations for the aesthetics of the modern world were laid. These years, in the world of art, were a time of revolution and much of that revolution was taking place in Paris. In her book *Paris France,* Gertrude Stein, who was living there, memorably stated the reality: "Paris was where the twentieth century was." It was the Paris of the Fauves, "the beasts," as they were dubbed, when painters such as Henri Matisse and André Derain shocked the fastidious by using vivid, pure colors—green, orange, black—colors that would be intrinsic to the Deco palette. It was the Paris where with his *Les demoiselles d'Avignon* of 1907, Pablo Picasso emblazoned Cubism on canvas, a Cubism which would profoundly affect the form of Deco architecture. It was the Paris to which in 1909 Serge Diaghilev brought the Ballets Russes, whose exotic Oriental-inspired sets and costumes by Bakst and Benois opened French designers to an eclectic spectrum of influences ranging from Indo-Chinese bibelots, African tribal gods, and Mayan pyramids to the ravishing treasures of King Tut's tomb, all of which would become a part of the Deco visual vocabulary. Finally, it was the Paris where, between 1911 and 1913, Auguste and Gustave Perret, working with Henry van de Velde, built the Théâtre des Champs-Élysées, which, in its minimalist classical details and its pioneering use of reinforced concrete, was a trail-blazing masterpiece of Art Deco architecture. The time lag between the inception of the Art Deco style and the exposition which paraded its presence in everything from wallpaper to bookbindings to pianos, to the flacons enclosing new scents, such as Guerlain's L'Heure Bleu, was the consequence of the bitter national rivalries and horrific blood-letting of the early 20th century.

On April 14, 1900, France inaugurated a grandiose Exposition Universelle in Paris which was essentially a celebration of Art Nouveau, the preeminent style of the turn of the century. That

style, which began dominating taste in the 1880s, eschewed the imitation of past modes of design such as Gothic and Classical, and was thus proclaimed "nouveau," new. It sought its inspiration in nature, in the curvilinear lines of the boughs of trees and in the foliate forms of flowers. And though the style had splendid practitioners elsewhere, such as Victor Horta in Brussels and Louis Sullivan and Louis Comfort Tiffany in the United States, the French looked upon Art Nouveau as theirs. Like the English Arts and Crafts movement which had preceded it, Art Nouveau rejected the machine-made products of the factory as vulgar—and many of them indeed were—and embraced instead the concept of the handcrafted, individually made object. Because it was French it also embraced the prodigal use of costly materials, rare woods, bronze, semiprecious gems. The style found supreme expression in the glass of Émile Gallé, the jewelry of René Lalique, the furniture of Louis Majorelle, and in the architecture of Hector Guimard, so perfectly exemplified by his sinuous cast-iron Paris Métro entrances.

The *Oasis* screen, by the ironsmith Edgar Brandt in collaboration with the architect-designer Henri Fabier, was one of the most admired objects in the 1925 Paris Exposition. Brandt (1880–1960) revolutionized ironworking by the use of new technology such as the pneumatic hammer, the metal press, and recently developed methods of fusing metals. The screen's palm fronds and tiered fountains became internationally recognized Art Deco images. (Private Collection).

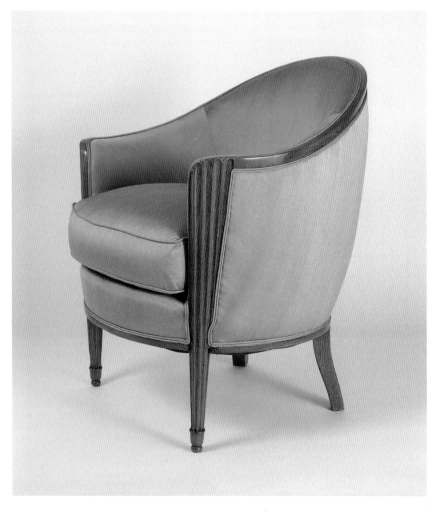

Mahogany "fan arm" chair by Jules Leleu, ca.1924. Respected for the extraordinarily high quality of his furniture, Leleu often used dark woods such as mahogany, Macassar ebony, and amboyna. He supplied the furniture for a dining room in the Elysée Palace, the official residence of the president of France. (Courtesy Maison Gerard, Ltd.)

But at the very moment of Art Nouveau's apogee, a bold challenge to all of its aesthetic tenets was launched from the new industrial and military behemoth east of the Rhine. For in Munich, in 1907, had been founded the Deutscher Werkbund, which proclaimed the radical concept that good design did not depend on individually made products, but that it could, with the input of artists, also be a product of the machine. The Werkbund soon had a huge membership, consisting of artists and architects, but, more significantly, the movement attracted Germany's leading manufacturers. It was quickly successful, not only aesthetically, but it also had a positive impact on the German economy, making German goods more attractive and desirable at home and abroad. A display of Werkbund products—machine-made furniture, cooking utensils, lamps—at the 1910 Paris Salon d'Automne was so popular that the police had to be called out to control the crowds. Art Nouveau suddenly appeared passé. This challenge from Germany in the field of design, an arena in which, since the 18th century, the French had reigned supreme, was a shock to the Gallic national psyche. In response, in 1912, the French government began planning a magnificent exposition that would reassert French mastery in every field of design. The exposition was slated to be held in Paris in 1915. History would ordain that in that year other more pressing events would absorb French energies, among them the appallingly deadly trench warfare of the Western Front.

Historians have a penchant for viewing epochs and even variations in style as though they fall into neatly defined categories and time slots which then, conveniently, lend themselves to being enclosed within the separate chapters of a book: " The Dark Ages" and "The Enlightenment," "The Victorian" and "The Edwardian" periods. Thus while the Art Deco exhibition in 1925, at first glance, represented a break with Art Nouveau and while there are indeed striking dissimilarities between the two aesthetics, it is important to be aware of their similarities, their continuity. Both were successors of the peerless 18th-century French *ébénistes, menuisiers,* and *bronziers* such as Jean-Henri Riesener, who fashioned a rolltop desk for Marie Antoinette with a mother-of-pearl veneer and mounts of gilt, silver, and steel, or Pierre Gouthière, who composed a perfume burner of red jasper and ormolu. A 1900 Art Nouveau cabinet of mahogany with gilded mounts and marquetry insets by Louis Majorelle and a 1920s Art Deco cabinet of Macassar ebony and silvered bronze by Émile-Jacques Ruhlmann share this common heritage. Art Deco, with its dependence on marvelously skilled craftsmen to fabricate its veneers of ebony, palmwood, jacaranda and calamander, its coverings of shagreen, snakeskin and pony, its wrought-iron lighting fixtures and its exquisite lacquers, was no more a style which readily lent itself to mass production than was Art Nouveau. And there is not infrequently in Art Deco design, whether it is the carved basket of flowers embellishing the back of a side chair by Paul Follot or the linear patterning on the surface of a small commode by Paul Iribe or the foliate images on a pair of lacquered wood and bronze panels by Armand-Albert Rateau, an element which bespeaks its debt to its predecessor style.

But while there are similarities between Art Nouveau and Art Deco, there is a wide aesthetic and psychological chasm separating the two. It is as evident as the gulf between an 1896 floor-length lavender silk afternoon dress by Charles Frederick Worth and a 1927 leg-revealing black jersey chemise by Coco Chanel. The essential difference is that while Art Nouveau proclaimed the "new," Art Deco embraced the "modern." This "modern" was exemplified by the machine in all its exciting and multifaceted manifestations, particularly those which seemed at last to offer man a chance to conquer space and time. Thus the significance of those graphic images which so exquisitely and precisely encapsulate the 1920s and 1930s: Charles Lindbergh landing solo the *Spirit of St. Louis* at Le Bourget; the *Twentieth Century Limited* slipping like quicksilver out of Grand Central; *Normandie* and *Mary* majestically moving up the Hudson; luminous white Pan American clippers departing LaGuardia for Europe in a spray of sea foam; the awesome vision of the airship *Hindenburg* sailing almost silently across the Atlantic toward America. The determination of Art Deco designers to express the pervasive presence of the machine in modern life lies behind their espousal of geometric forms: the triangle, the circle, the square, the octagon. These were, in reality, artistic representations of the ball bearings, the cogs and wheels of the factory itself. Likewise, a wish to evince in stationary objects, ranging from platinum-diamond clips to stone and steel skyscrapers, that sense of movement so intrinsic to the era spawned many of the most prevalent Art Deco motifs: chevrons, lighting bolts, zigzags, parallel lines, and overlapping images.

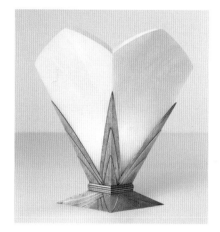

The impact of the 1925 Paris Exposition on the United States and particularly on New York City was profound and rapid. There is a certain irony in this, for the United States, even though it had been invited to participate and had been assigned a premier location for its pavilion near those of France's other World War allies, Britain, Belgium, and Italy, declined the offer. The truth was that the Secretary of Commerce, Herbert Hoover, felt that America could not meet the requirement that all displays at the Exposition should be unreservedly modern. (It is impossible to know whether the Secretary and his advisors considered turning to Frank Lloyd Wright and other Prairie School architects who had been designing daringly modern buildings, furni-

In 1928, the rector of one of Manhattan's oldest churches, St. Mark's-in-the-Bowery of 1799, commissioned Frank Lloyd Wright to design three glass and steel apartment towers which would rise from the churchyard at Tenth Street and Second Avenue. The Depression killed the project, but the avant-garde architecture of the proposed towers makes it clear that the United States could have indeed constructed a pavilion at the 1925 Exposition which would have been unabashedly modern. (Private Collection.)

ture, glass, and fabrics for more than two decades.) Hoover, though, did perceive the importance of the Exposition and quickly created a commission to visit Paris and prepare a report for American manufacturers. The irresistible combination of the allure of the French capital, the widespread affluence in America at the time which made transatlantic travel feasible, and the sense that the nation needed a new style to supplant the prevailing Beaux Arts canon, led to an astonishing response to Hoover's proposal. In the summer of 1925, eighty-seven delegates from organizations as varied as the American Institute of Architects, the Society of Interior Designers, the Silk Association of America, the United Women's Wear, the New York State Department of Education, the Metropolitan Museum of Art, and the *New York Times* passed between Pierre Patout's 10 pylons which marked the Exposition's place de la Concorde entrance. Their various reports and published articles made Art Deco the *dernier cri* in fashion and furniture, in textiles and graphics, and, most significantly, in architecture.

Tens of thousands of other Americans also visited Paris that radiant summer of 1925 and when they returned on the *Leviathan* or *Majestic* or *Berengaria* or *Paris*, many quickly sought something tastefully different from the gilded Louis and the barleytwist-leg Jacobean revivals which were the mainstays of upper-middle-class Yankee décor. New York firms were quick to oblige them. Indeed, F. Schumacher & Co., one of the leading purveyors of textiles, boasted a complete Art Deco chamber in its West 40th Street showrooms which displayed modern fabrics while the Paris Exposition was in progress. The conception of Pierre Pozier, the man in charge of Schumacher's product development, the room—with metalwork by Edgar Brandt, pottery by Jean Luce, and glass by René Lalique—was constructed in France, disassembled, shipped to New York, and then reassembled. Among the avant-garde textiles displayed in it was one woven of the new man-made fiber, rayon, with a metallic leaf design inspired by Brandt's *Oasis* screen, which could be seen at that very moment in Paris.

As early as 1927 Brooklyn's Abraham & Straus department store promoted an entire living room furnished with pieces by the innovative Viennese-born Paul T. Frankl, including one of his skyscraper-inspired bookcases. The next year Lord & Taylor was showing furniture by the foremost French designers, including Ruhlmann, Louis Süe, and Andre Maré, while Macy's offered a choice of rooms by French design firms such as Leleu and D. I. M., but also some by Americans like the New York architect Eugene Schoen. The grand dame of New York department stores, B. Altman & Co., not only mounted an Émile-Jacques Ruhlmann exhibition in 1928, but commissioned pieces directly from the cutting-edge French designer. Signaling its awareness of this dramatic change in taste, W. & J. Sloane, which specialized in traditional furniture and curtain and upholstery materials, daringly featured 29 cubistic patterns in woven and printed fabrics by the American Ruth Reeves, who had worked in Paris with Fernand Léger.

There was one major other than the United States which did not participate in the 1925 Paris exposition and that was Germany. Now not only a feared commercial competitor, but a defeated enemy as well, the Germans claimed that their invitation arrived too late for them

Paul Follot's *Leaves*, a daring combination of rayon and metallic threads, was inspired by Edgar Brandt's *Oasis* screen (shown on page 3). *Leaves* was used as a wall frieze in F. Schumacher & Co.'s Art Deco New York showroom, which was open during the run of the Paris Exposition. (F. Schumacher & Co.)

to organize a worthy display. As a result, the work of the Bauhaus, founded in 1919 by Walter Gropius, which was the aesthetic heir of the Deutscher Werkbund, was not on view on the banks of the Seine in 1925. One notable German architect, though, was represented. Peter Behrens designed a faceted glass greenhouse for the courtyard of the Austrian Pavilion which was enthusiastically praised by the young American architect, Ely Jacques Kahn. But Behrens was there only at the invitation of the man in charge of the pavilion, Josef Hoffmann.

Thus there is more than a grain of nationalism in the mix which fueled the bitter animosity between Art Deco and the architectural style which grew out of the Bauhaus. For while Deco was profoundly influenced by the Viennese Secession, by Italian Futurism, and by German Expressionism, the moderne style, as Art Deco was originally labeled, was, after 1925, looked upon as something wholly French. On the other hand, "The International Style," a term coined by the American architect Philip Johnson in 1932 to characterize the work of those influenced by the Bauhaus, was inescapably German. Its advocacy of severe functionalism, its repudiation of ornament, its desire to dematerialize walls by constructing them of glass, and its espousal of naked structure are prime articles of faith of the Bauhaus and of the Bauhaus architects, such as Gropius and Mies van der Rohe, who emigrated to the United States in the 1930s. This "skin and bones construction," as Mies characterized it, had no appeal for Art Deco architects.

Art Deco was always a thorn in the side of those who advocated the International Style as the only valid modern style. The theoreticians of academe found it impossible to neatly categorize it and at times were reduced to such unhappy solutions as calling its practitioners "avant-garde traditionalists." It was not theoretical in the way that only a German-born school of architecture could be theoretical. It was also emphatically not political, possessing no sacred credo such as Gropius's famed 1919 Bauhaus "Manifesto" which demanded a new way of building "without the class distinctions which raise an arrogant barrier between craftsman and artist." As a consequence, it was often dismissed as an architecture without significance. Typically, in the catalogue of the Museum of Modern Art's influential 1932 show, "Modern Architecture—International Exhibition," the Museum's Director, Alfred Barr, made it clear that Art Deco was unworthy of being seen in the Museum. For Barr, like for many architectural purists, it was "merely another way of decorating surfaces."

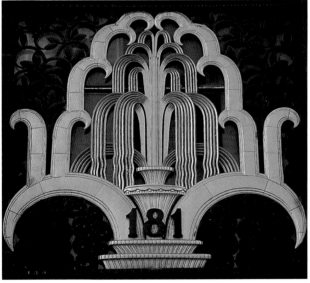

In the 1920s Edgar Brandt established a New York branch of his ironworking business called Ferrobrandt. The firm was commissioned in 1925 by Cheney Brothers, silk manufacturers, to create a pair of magnificent entrances for its showroom at the southeast corner of Madison Avenue and 34th Street. The result is one of New York's truly great Art Deco monuments. (Photographs by John Cadenhead.)

The 1,030-foot-long *Normandie*, at the time the world's largest ship and the pride of the French Line, sails down the Hudson on June 6, 1935, on her first return voyage to France. (Private Collection.)

Undoubtedly a prime source of the animosity of International Style advocates toward Art Deco was the fact that Deco was what the International Style longed to be, mass modern. It appeared in the United States in the 1920s at the very moment when, in New York and elsewhere, commercial interests were demanding structures which would express the new spirit of the age in forms which were attractive, opulent, and humane.

Art Deco provided the perfect answer. It was an ideal transition from the extravagant Beaux Arts idiom of the previous generation which had given the city beloved buildings such as the Public Library on Fifth Avenue at 42nd Street and the Plaza Hotel on Central Park South. Not freighted with theories which touted the morality of austerity or with political screeds better

suited to a defeated angst-ridden continental empire than to an optimistic democratic America, Art Deco was eager to display its delight in the sumptuous by the use of rich materials—colored terra-cotta, mosaics, vitrolite, aluminum leaf, bronzed glass—to make shop windows that were irresistible, hotel lobbies that were spaces of effulgent grandeur, office building entrances that would wake King Tut, and boîtes with the kick of a straight-up gin martini. And though there was some evolution of the style toward a more restrained mode in the final years of the 1930s, between the two world wars, it was Deco under its various names—"Modernistic," "Streamline," "Jazz Modern"— which vivified New York's aesthetics and crowned the city's skyline with stars.

In January of 1933, the noted author and professor of architecture at Columbia University, Talbot Hamlin, published an article in *The American Architect* entitled "The International Style Lacks the Essence of Great Architecture," which unreservedly came down on the side of Art Deco:

It is not quantitative functionalism that is at the root of great architecture. It is not obtuse intellectual content of any kind. It is not conformity to any theory. It is never the result of labored and self-conscious puritanism. It is never a denial of the joy in life . . . . Great architecture had disciplines that are more stimuli than inhibitions. It can be helped, but never created, by structural expression; yet structural expression carried to the limit would often spoil it. . . . The root of great architecture is like the root of any created beauty, deep in the matrix of human consciousness. It is spontaneity, delight in form. It is superfluity— almost always a sense of "more than enough." It is the play of creative minds that makes living and building a delight. Can it be that the International Style has never learned how to play?

In the 1920s and 1930s, with its urbanity, its sophistication, its wit, and, above all, with its unabashed advocacy of beauty, Art Deco helped to make New York City and the lives of those who dwelt there a delight. And can anyone say that the architectural style which produced Radio City Music Hall did not know how to play?

# *Announcing*
# 20TH
## THE NEW *Streamlined*
## CENTURY LIMITED

. . . . . *Starting June 15, 1938*

**16 HOURS** between **NEW YORK** and **CHICAGO**

**The First All-Room Train in America**

# ARRIVING IN STYLE

Manhattan welcomed into its very heart two of the supreme symbols of the Art Deco Age, the French Line's *Normandie* and the New York Central's *Twentieth Century Limited*. Rising beside the deep estuary of the Hudson with its dredged channel that runs from Ellis Island to 59th Street, a channel 40 feet deep and up to 2,800 feet wide, New York could tether the mightiest liners on its very doorstep, and dock them in the shadow of skyscrapers as high as the ships were long. It is a privilege shared by only a handful of cities—Rio de Janeiro, Sydney, Hong Kong. Passengers to Paris did not disembark beneath the Eiffel Tower but at Le Havre or Cherbourg, and London offered only the nautical scraps of Southampton. This is not insignificant, for the sleek horses of the sea in their watery paddocks, which in the glory days of ocean travel extended from the Battery northward to West 72nd Street, were truly a part of Manhattan's cityscape. They were a part of it the way the new streamlined *Broadway Limited* tunneling beneath the Hudson into the Beaux Arts glory of Pennsylvania Station and the drop-dead chic *Twentieth Century* gliding into Grand Central were a part of it. Thomas Wolfe, in his 1935 novel, *Of Time and the River*, observed how the sound of the liners infiltrated New York: "And there are ships there! Have we not heard the ships there? (Have we not heard the great ships going down the river? Have we not heard the great ships putting out to sea?)"

All significant design is fraught with history, for it is, like the honey of bees, never the spontaneous production of a single moment, but the gathering of a multitude of essences from a field of flowers. It would be difficult to name an artifact which more vividly mirrored the rent of the fabric of civilization caused by the First World War than the ocean liner. To look at photographs of the pre-1914 liners, particularly those launched just before the Guns of August began their deadly cannonade, is to view images of a world for whom the bell has already begun to toll. There is, in those ships, a startling disconnect between their advanced engineering and

ABOVE  The French Line not only sailed the most beautiful Deco ships between New York and Cherbourg, but also produced the most sensational posters, such as this 1935 one celebrating the *Normandie*. (Private Collection.)

OPPOSITE  In advertising the new *Twentieth Century Limited* the New York Central boldly emphasized the similarity of its mighty J-3a Hudson locomotives to rocket ships. This underscored the reason for the expensive 1938 redesign of the train, which was to lure ridership back to the rails by selling it as a modern way to travel. To further dramatize the power of the locomotives, the designer responsible for the Deco *Twentieth Century*, Henry Dreyfuss, had lights installed above their brightly finished drive wheels to clearly reveal their awesome power as the *Century* dashed through the night. (Private Collection.)

their backward-looking décor, a disconnect which would not be bridged until the appearance of Art Deco.

The British vessels of the era strove to carry the stately homes of England to sea. This decorative ploy was not without a certain commercial logic; it appealed not only to their own upper classes but to many wealthy Americans who early in life in their prep schools and colleges had been inoculated with Anglophilia. Typically, White Star Line's 45,000-ton *Olympic,* launched in 1910—sister ship of the *Titanic,* launched in 1911—was a veritable architectural tour of Britain—a bit of Robert Adam, a bit of Queen Anne, a bit of Jacobean—to the point that one English critic wrote, with some asperity: "The tourist will be spared the round of visits through these islands, for he will become familiarized with our historical architectural treasures while crossing the ocean by rambling through his temporary floating home." A Cunard publicity release which preceded the launching reported deadpan, without the slightest awareness of the pitfalls of self-parody: "As regards the decorations, a faint echo only of Tudor times is found. . . . From this we pass to the days of Sir Anthonie van Dyck and Inigo Jones, but the periods of domestic architecture and decorations most completely illustrated in the ship are those which lie between the Restoration of Charles II and the middle of the reign of George III." The passage brings to mind Elsie de Wolfe's riposte to a pretentious woman who announced to the renowned decorator: "This is my Louis XV room" "What makes you think so?" Elsie shot back. The ships of the late 1920s and 1930s would have to appeal to a very different aesthetic.

If Cunard and White Star sought to carry the resplendence of Chatsworth and Badminton to the shores of Britain's former colonies, the Hamburg-Amerikanische Packetfahrt-Actien-Gesellschaft (the Hamburg-America or Amerika Line) and Norddeutscher Lloyd (North German Lloyd Company) were determined to display something quite different, the might of the new German Empire. After all, Germany, as a nation, was a very recent creation constituted only after the defeat of France in 1870. The economic success of German passenger ships in the 19th century, like that of their British competitors, had, in no small part, been based on the constant flow of immigrants westward across the Atlantic. Out of Bremen and Hamburg the German ships each year carried thousands of Germans, Scandinavians, Poles, and Russians headed to the American states of the Midwest, just as Cunard and White Star sailed from Liverpool and Queenstown with their steerage packed with English, Irish, Welsh, and Scots seeking opportunities in the New World. The virtual disappearance of this traffic in the 1920s would change ship travel forever.

The atmosphere of the German ships of the 1860s and 1870s had been very gemütlich, reminiscent, American travelers said, of some small hotel near Heidelberg or Munich, but now, with its growing wealth and its industrial power, Wilhelmine Germany demanded that its liners underscore its new place in the sun. Suddenly the shipowners of Bremen and Hamburg, having learned all they needed to know from the British engineers they had hired from the yards on the Tyne and Clyde and with almost unlimited government support, were prepared to make a reality of the haughty motto of Hamburg-Amerika: "Mein Feld Ist Die Welt" (My Field Is the World). Thus the

awesome 649-foot-long *Kaiser Wilhelm der Grosse,*
launched in 1897, was more than a ship, to the British it
was a weapon. Carrying 2,300 passengers at an astonishing 21 knots, the *Kaiser Wilhelm der Grosse* easily captured
from the British the prestigious Blue Riband for the
fastest transatlantic crossing. Beneath its four tall funnels, Germany's preeminent marine designer, Johannes
Poppe, created public rooms higher than any ever before
seen on a ship, rooms that, with their carved caryatides,
acres of stained glass, and prairies of gilded rococo plaster, seemed lifted bodily from the new palaces rising in
Berlin. "Very late North German Lloyd" became a phrase
of both wonder and derision.

While through the 1890s the British and German lines
grew ever larger, Compagnie Générale Transatlantique,
the French Line, sailed a different course. Its *La Touraine,*
for example, the last great liner to carry a full set of sails
(in case the engines failed) emphasized quiet luxury
aimed at the well-to-do, matchless cuisine, and an entire
ship free of the disturbing presence of poor immigrants.
This last amenity was one of the reasons for the popularity of the French Line with Americans, for the French
had never been involved in the mass transportation of
immigrants to North America. When asked why not, an
official of the Compagnie Générale replied with typical
Gallic insouciance: "People don't leave Paris; they come
to it." This highly profitable trade was one of the reasons

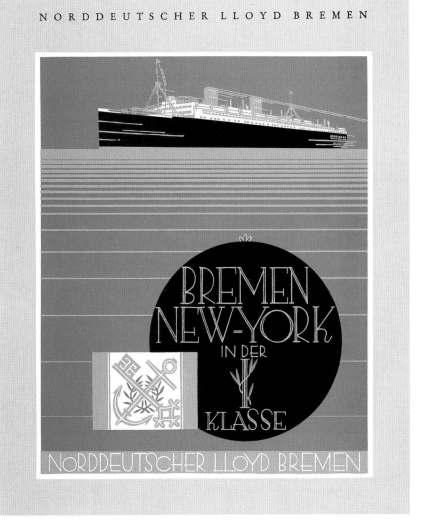

Launched in August, 1928, the North German
Lloyd's *Bremen* was a key part of Germany's push
to regain its "rightful" place on the seas. The interior design of the ship left behind the overstuffed
comforts of past German ships for a sleek modernity which caught the attention of the world's other
steamship lines. (Private Collection.)

for the astounding growth in the size of British and German ships, but the presence of the immigrants disturbed sensitive Americans. Muriel Gardiner, née Morris, heiress of a Chicago meat-
packing dynasty, tellingly recalled the reality in her 1983 memoir, *Code Name Mary:* "When in
1910 my family took me to Europe, I looked down every day from our enclosed first-class deck
to the open steerage deck below. Even in rainy or rough weather when the waves were pouring
over the lower, open space, crowds would gather there—men, women in their black shawls, and
children of all ages. To this day, the very word 'steerage' gives me a sick feeling."

But in 1912, national pride and an increasing concern at the growing dominance on the sea of
the Teutonic powerhouse led the French Line to launch the *France.* At a mere 24,000 tons it was
smaller than its German and British rivals, but what it lacked in tonnage, the *France* made up in
élan. The ship's décor carried Parisian Belle Epoque opulence to new heights. A commentator

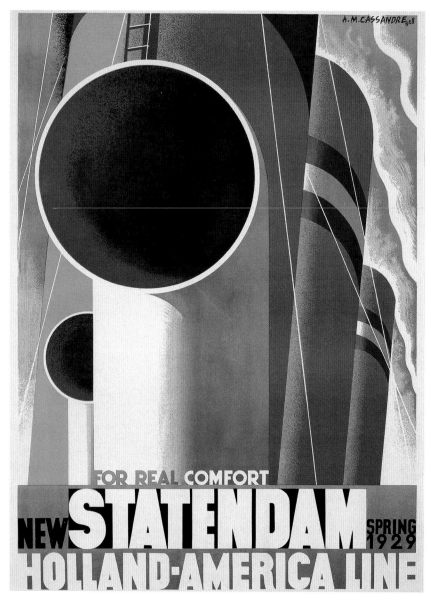

FOR REAL COMFORT
NEW STATENDAM SPRING 1929
HOLLAND-AMERICA LINE

Some Americans preferred to skip the over-the-top grandeur of the British, French, and Italian lines and opt instead for the more democratic ambience of ships of the Holland-American Line. The *Statendam*, launched in 1929, shown in this poster exemplifying the Deco love of geometry, was a favorite. (Private Collection.)

said that all of the 18th century seemed to have been swept into the *France*. First class cabins had canopied beds which, because of the vessel's tendency to roll like a drunken sailor, often collapsed upon startled sleepers; the main salon sported paneling from the Château of the Comte de Toulouse and everywhere portraits of Louis XIV, Madame de Maintenon, and other French worthies gazed down upon the contented passengers. An English spy for Cunard reported that, while the *France* was beautifully decorated, it was unsuitable for English travelers because "no notice was taken of the Sabbath." It was easy to forget the Sabbath on a ship whose cellars were filled with Château Margaux and Château Haut-Brion and which proudly announced that before every voyage 18 barrels of pâté de foie gras were wheeled aboard.

The First World War would change everything. When, at the beginning of the 1920s, the British and French lines relaunched their refurbished ships, like the *Olympic*, which had been used as troop transports, and their war prizes seized from the defeated Germans, like the *Imperator*, renamed the *Berengaria*, and the *Bismarck*, rechristened the *Majestic*, their white and gold palm-filled salons suddenly struck a false note. "It was like the Breakers at sea," a young Vanderbilt, referring to his family "cottage" in Newport, quipped of the *Olympic*. And there was another great divide between the prewar and postwar worlds. In 1921 the United States Congress had passed the Emergency Quota Act, dramatically restricting immigration. From an average of 700,000 annually in the years immediately preceding the war, emigration quickly dropped to a few thousand. The gigantic German and British ships constructed to carry the lucrative emigrant trade now sailed with their vast steerage sections eerily silent. And while the interior design of one of the first postwar Cunarders, the *Carinthia*, did not look back to the Belle Epoque, it did look toward Iberia. Indeed the *Carinthia*'s public rooms displayed a Spanish Revival style akin to that found in the new haciendas of Santa Barbara, California, and Palm Beach, Florida.

There were no aesthetic recollections of Iberia or of the vanished courts of Europe in the black-hulled, three-funneled, 43,000-ton ship the French sailed into New York harbor in the spring of

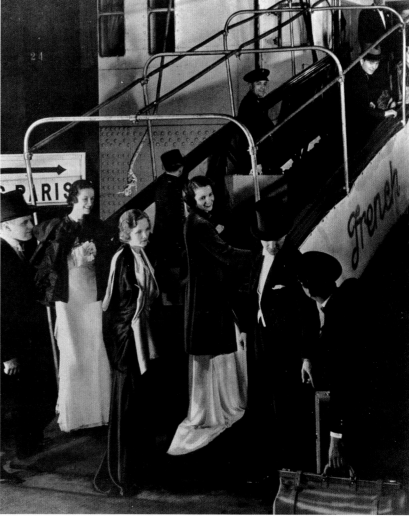

"THE LONGEST GANGPLANK
IN THE WORLD"

Weekly Express Service between
New York, London and Paris

French Line

Compagnie Générale Transatlantique
New York-Paris

ABOVE LEFT It was not unusual in the 1920s and 1930s for passengers, particularly for those traveling first class, to take their cars to Europe. This 1927 drawing shows an automobile being swung up to be deposited below decks the day before sailing. (Drawing by Laurence Fellows, *Vogue*,© 2004 Condé Nast Publications.)

ABOVE RIGHT Passengers boarding the French Line's *Paris*. In the days of midnight sailing, evening dress was *de rigueur*. (American Architectural Archives.)

LEFT The concept that once you stepped aboard a French ship you were in Paris was a staple of French Line advertising. (Private Collection.)

The *Ile de France* was handsome without being grand, comfortable without being overstuffed, class-conscious without living by exclusions. Yet no one would ever adequately account for her matchless power to attract the talented and youthful, the stylish and the eminent; or say why it was that one ship, neither better nor bigger than a dozen others on the same Atlantic thoroughfare, would win for herself unprecedented affection and loyalty. Names that appeared again and again on her tasseled and embossed passenger lists provide an index to her appeal, and perhaps to her character: Arturo Toscanini, Maurice Chevalier, Will Rogers, Maude Adams, John D. Rockefeller, Jascha Heifetz, Bernard Baruch, Argentina, Virgil Thomson, Ivar Kreuger, Jeanette MacDonald, Tallulah Bankhead, Gloria Swanson, Barbara Hutton, Helen Morgan, Pola Negri, Feodor Chaliapin, Samuel Goldwyn.

John Malcolm Brinnin's words above from *Grand Luxe* brilliantly capture the enduring attraction of the *Ile de France* of 1927. (Private Collection.)

1927. The difference between the *Ile de France* and the White Star's *Olympic* was the difference between a flapper sporting a paillette-covered sheath and a dowager encased in bombazine. The first all-new liner launched since the war, the interiors of the *Ile* were the product of a revolutionary concept. Rather than having one designer like Johannes Poppe do all of the interiors, the French Line commissioned a team of craftsmen to produce spaces of the very highest quality, spaces which would reflect the Roaring Twenties. Some of those who had a hand in creating the interiors of the *Ile de France*—Lalique and Ruhlmann, for instance—were already famous, but here, for the first time in America, appeared artists and designers whose names would become legendary in the archives of Art Deco: Alfred Janniot, who would create friezes for Rockefeller Center; Raymond Subes, one of the supreme Art Deco innovators in the use of steel and aluminum; and Adalbert Szabo, whose groundbreaking iron and frosted glass lamps would have a profound influence on Donald Deskey.

In its restrained grand entrance foyer, paneled in shades of gray Pyrenees marble and lit by Lalique fixtures, and in Le Salon Mixte— daringly welcoming both men and women—with its moderne statues by Janniot, its octagon mirrors by Subes, and its silvered bronze boiserie by Ruhlmann, the *Ile de France* introduced the world to *le style paquebot*. Now, in a breathtaking reversal, instead of the palaces of Berlin or the country houses of Gloucestershire being floated out upon the Atlantic, the salons of the *Ile de France* would come ashore to inspire the lobbies of hotels like New York's Waldorf-Astoria and Cincinnati's Netherland Plaza, as well as some of America's most extraordinary commercial spaces, including Chicago's Diana Court and Rockefeller Center's International Building.

It was not only the physical presence of the dazzling new décor of the *Ile de France* which made it one of the most beloved ships in transatlantic ferry service history, but it was also what that décor represented. In the years between the First and Second World Wars, that is, the 1920s and 1930s, the ancient friendship between France and the United States, a friendship redolent with revered names such as Lafayette and Rochambeau, had been given, as it were, a booster shot by the camaraderie of the two nations in the Great War itself. That camaraderie has been forever preserved in songs such as George M. Cohan's "Over There" and in phrases such as: "How you gonna keep 'em down on the farm, after they've seen Paree?" The French Line played to this appeal with one of the most brilliant slogans in advertising history: "The Longest Gangplank in the World." Once you stepped aboard, you were in Paris.

Ironically, it was the United States Congress which gave the *Ile de France* and other French ships a distinct advantage over their U.S. competitors. With the passage of the Volstead Act, which went into effect in 1920, all American vessels, including the gargantuan *Leviathan* seized from Germany, became "dry." And while Britain did not participate in the so-called "noble experiment," its ships were better known for their stately grandeur than for their raffishness. Two of the *Ile*'s amenities emphasized by the French Line were its 56-foot bar, the longest in the world, and its Café Terrasse, which, the Line promised, was the equivalent of the best sidewalk café in Paris. As any smart American headed to the City of Light knew, once the 12-mile limit was reached, Champagne flowed on the *Ile de France* the way Coca-Cola flowed in Atlanta, Georgia.

In 1920's America, the America of "Silent Cal" Coolidge and of pervasive provincialism, the America of which H. L. Mencken said, "If you heave an egg out of a Pullman window, you will probably hit a Fundamentalist," Paris was irresistible. In her 1982 memoir of her mother and father, Sara and Gerald Murphy, leaders of the American colony in France, Honoria Murphy Donnelly explains why her parents left their homeland: "I can speak only for the Murphys, but their discontent had to do with an absence of cultural stimulation in America, a philistine attitude." "It was not what Paris gave you," Gertrude Stein, who lived there, observed, "but what it did not take away." A phalanx of talented Americans—Ernest Hemingway, Edith Wharton, Man Ray, Scott Fitzgerald, Josephine Baker, to name but a few—unreservedly agreed with Miss Stein.

There are words which begin their lives in the thoroughfares of commerce and move on to encapsulate the

Among the most sensational examples of *le style paquebot* is the lobby of the Netherland Plaza in Cincinnati, Ohio. Designed in 1931 by Walter Alschlager and the theatrical designer George Unger, the lobby is a glittering lesson in French Art Deco's love of exotic materials—rare woods and marbles—and its fascination with non-European motifs—in this case, Egyptian. (Private Collection.)

very essence of all that is incomparable and glamorous. Ritz, Rolls, and Pullman must be noted and, of course, *Normandie*. The first ocean liner to exceed 1,000 feet, she weighed an awesome 83,000 tons and carried, when officers and crew were counted, 3,326 souls, and her four propellers could drive her across the Atlantic at a record-breaking 30 knots an hour. The ship's remarkably beautiful lines were due in no small part to a brilliant design innovation. Whereas for more than a century liners had been built with straight or plumb bows, *Normandie* sported a graceful clipper-ship bow, the creation of the Russian-born naval architect, Vladimir Yourkevitch. This revolutionary innovation allowed *Normandie* to make the same speed as the *Queen Mary*, using one-fifth less horsepower.

ABOVE The *Normandie* departing Le Havre on her maiden voyage, May 29, 1935. (Roger-Viollet.)

At 6:30 p.m. on May 29, 1935, to the strains of "La Marseillaise" played by a band on her promenade deck, the *Normandie* eased out of Le Havre on her maiden voyage headed for New York. More than 50,000 spectators cheered the strikingly elegant ship with its three black and red dashingly raked funnels on her way. "The vessel," reported *The Christian Science Monitor,* "represented a whole nation's joyful pride." The *Monitor* was correct, for the *Normandie* was seen by the French Line as a floating show house of the most *à la page* French taste, an alluring advertisement for French luxury goods at a time when the worldwide depression was drying up the market for costly furniture and fabrics, for couture gowns and vintage wines, for crystal and silver. The roster of prominent artists and decorators which the line recruited made the *Normandie* a veritable Xanadu of dazzling Deco design. Among the ship's spectacular treasures were Jules Leleu's deluxe Trouville Suite with blond ash furniture and walls lined in ivory-colored Moroccan leather; the Rouen Suite by the firm of Dominique whose walls were of black lacquer and pigskin; Edgar Brandt's superb glass and iron lighting fixtures; Jean Mayodon's crackled glass tiles; sculptors Jan and Joel Martel's gold cubistic altar in the chapel; Émile-Jacques Ruhlmann's grand piano; and Jean Dunand's chess tables of *coquille d'oeuf* (broken eggshell) lacquer.

The *Normandie's* split uptakes, a brilliant but expensive innovation which removed the massive funnels from the ship's center, allowed the vessel to be opened up from stem to stern, permitting public rooms to be unobstructed spaces of staggering dimensions. The opening theme was sounded by the main embarkation hall. Designed by the architects Jean Patout and Henri Pacon, its 2½-deck-high walls were sheathed in creamy Algerian onyx, with, at one end, a mounted knight—the world's largest cloisonné fabrication—which subtly reminded one and all that, in 1066, the Normans had conquered England. At the other end a pair of 15-foot-high gilded bronze doors, embellished with vignettes of significant Normandy locales—Rouen, Caen, Le Havre—led into the dining room. This vast silver and gold chamber, 305 feet long, 46 feet wide, and three decks high, was one of the most astonishing spaces ever created for a ship. Its 150 tables comfortably seated 1,700 diners and every appointment, from the Daum crystal to the Christofle silver, proclaimed the perfection of modern French taste. This windowless air-conditioned hall—one of the first on a ship to have that amenity—was lit by thirty-eight 16-foot-high wall sconces and twelve tall opaque glass torchères by Lalique making the room appear to be illuminated by frozen fountains.

The 110-foot by 85-foot grand salon eschewed the restrained palette of the dining room for a color scheme that was decidedly La Vie en Rose. Its red lacquer tables and its chairs upholstered in rose-colored Aubusson

TOP The *Normandie's* smoking room was decorated with lacquered panels by Jean Dunand depicting scenes of hunting and fishing in an "Egyptian" style. (Private Collection.)

BOTTOM The grand salon of the *Normandie* served as an afternoon tea room, a cocktail lounge, and, late in the evening, a nightclub. (Private Collection.)

tapestry designed by F. Gaudissart, whose theme was the flowers of France's overseas colonies, gave it a rubescent glow appropriate for its alternative use as a ballroom cum nightclub. And a French Line brochure made it clear that when the grand salon's rug was rolled up late at night, couples wouldn't find themselves fox-trotting on linoleum. The dance floor beneath was an exact replica of the parquetry in the throne room at Fontainebleau. The walls of the grand salon were ornamented with one of the supreme 1930s Art Deco assemblages, four silvered and gilt *verre églomisé* murals by Jean Dupas depicting the history of navigation. Alastair Duncan, in his invaluable book *Art Deco,* perfectly expresses the memorable quality of this rare chamber: "The lavish ivory and olive tones on vivid orange-red and grey grounds, set against the gold and silver leaf of the murals produced an image of splendor unrivalled in the 'floating palaces' of any other nation."

Though Ludwig Bemelmans, who was a passenger on the *Normandie*'s maiden voyage, opined that she "leaned to excess," the creator of Madeline was in a distinct minority. When, on June 3, the *Normandie*—already flying the Blue Riband won for crossing the Atlantic at a record-breaking 30 knots an hour—reached New York, she was received as a conquering hero. Planes circled overhead, fireboats spewed sprays into the air, a hundred vessels whistled their greetings, while the *Normandie*'s 620-pound three-note whistle responded with its own powerful salutation. It is estimated that 10,000 people had gathered in Fort Hamilton Park, Brooklyn, with another 100,000 in nearby areas; 5,000 crowded onto Bedloe's Island beneath the Statue of Liberty; while more than 30,000 were crammed into Battery Park for a view of France's latest gift to the New World. At her dock on West 48th Street, thousands queued up to make a contribution to the Seamen's Fund which would allow them to tour this, as it was being called, "Versailles upon the Sea." The ship's most important passenger, Madame Albert Lebrun, wife of the French President, was given a reception at the Waldorf-Astoria, where Mayor Fiorello LaGuardia presented her with a silver cigarette case. The next day Madame Lebrun visited President and Mrs. Franklin D. Roosevelt.

The *New York Times* was impressed: "The immense proportions of some of the salons and the glamourousness of their décor overwhelmed some, made them feel like mice in a cathedral, but did provide a gorgeous setting." There can be no doubt that the setting was indeed "gorgeous" and made the *Normandie* the ship in which one was most likely to cross with Maurice Chevalier or Cary Grant or Marlene Dietrich. And it is also true that its scale and luminous perfection made it both wonderful and wondrous. "You feel aboard the *Normandie*," Arnold Gingrich, editor of *Esquire*, said, "not at home on it . . . home was never like this."

Curiously, the stock market crash of October 1929, which triggered the Great Depression of the 1930s—called in England "the Great Slump"—facilitated the completion of the ship which would signal Britain's entry into the world of nautical Deco design. Labeled "Hull 534," the vessel being built at John Brown's yard on the Clyde was about 80 percent complete when work was stopped in late 1931. The embarrassing reality was that Cunard, losing an estimated 20 million dollars a year, simply could not afford to complete the project. Since White Star was in equally dire straits, the financial crisis gave the government an opportunity to accomplish what it had long desired, a

merger of Cunard and White Star to create a single strong British presence in the North Atlantic to compete against the sleek new German ships, *Bremen* and *Europa*. The offer by Prime Minister Neville Chamberlin of 9 ½ million pounds, 3 million being earmarked for the completion of Hull 534, did the trick. Work resumed in April of 1934 and six months later, in the presence of King George V and his consort, for whom the ship was to be named, the new Cunard–White Star Line launched the *Queen Mary*. The King aptly described the vessel as "The stateliest ship in the world."

While the decorators who worked on the *Mary* did not match the innovative brilliance of the men who crafted her hull, superstructure, and engines, they did strive to banish the "stately homes" ambience favored by their predecessors. In fact, Cunard sent a spy to report on the new *Normandie* in her shipyard across the Channel. This nascent attempt at an English modernity did not always succeed. *The Architect and Building News* said of the liner's interiors, "The General Effect is one of mild but expensive vulgarity." And in *Brideshead Revisited*, the waspish novelist Evelyn Waugh has the painter Charles Ryder complain: "I turned into some of the halls of the ship, which were huge without any splendor." But much of the criticism was more clever than fair. Under the direction of Arthur Davis, who had been a partner of the fabled Charles Mewes, an Alsatian architect who had before his death in 1913 given the Hamburg-America's ships the glitter to be found in his Paris and London Ritz hotels, produced a number of rooms that per-

65
PULLMAN
SLEEPERS WOULD BE
NEEDED TO MOVE THE
2075 PASSENGERS WHICH
THE "QUEEN MARY" CAN CARRY
ON ONE TRIP ~ 15 COACHES
WOULD BE NEEDED TO MOVE
THE CREW, ~ COMPARED TO

The 200 PEOPLE THAT WERE
PASSENGERS AND CREW ON THE
FIRST CUNARDER "BRITANNIA"

TOP The main lounge of the *Queen Mary* exemplified Art Deco held in check by a British dedication to comfort combined with stateliness. (Private Collection.)

BOTTOM To underscore the enormous size of the *Queen Mary*, Cunard–White Star issued a "Book of Comparisons." The dazzling difference between the *Britannia* of 1840 and the new *Queen* of 1936 could not fail to impress. (Private Collection.)

fectly expressed an elegant, reserved British modernity. The *Mary's* two-story main lounge, with veneered oval wood columns, overscaled Deco-inspired club chairs, handsome small cocktail tables clearly influenced by the work of French designers such as Subes and Ruhlmann, and circular lighting fixtures in the style of Jean Perzel, had a subtle, complex appeal which brought passengers back time and time again. The noted steamship historian John Malcolm Brinnin sums up the secret of the *Mary's* success in his masterful study of transatlantic liners, *Grand Luxe:* "While she would eventually be categorized as one of the most celebrated artifacts of what would soon be known as Depression Modern, the *Queen Mary* in her time continued to be endowed by her international clientele with a smartness, an in-group exclusivity unapproached in the later phases of transatlantica." That appeal was at one with the new decorating scheme, carried out by Oswald Milne, in London's Claridge's Hotel, bringing to the grand old caravansary Cubist-inspired upholstery, silvered cornices, and glass panels by Lalique. The *Mary's* Deco-inspired modernism was best expressed in the cocktail bar of the forward observation lounge. The room was, from its round tables, curving bar, and tall red-enameled light-filled urns to the jazzy pattern on its Ruboleum floor, an unabashed symphony of Deco circularity. But just to make it clear that this was indubitably an English ship, the mural above the bar was no ersatz Léger or Braque, but a realistic depiction of all classes dancing together in a London street in 1935 to celebrate King George V's Silver Jubilee.

If, by the second half of the 1930s, those coming to New York by sea were given a dazzling display of Art Deco, so too would those coming by rail over the two preeminent lines serving the city, the Pennsylvania and the New York Central. But both were slow to replace their comfortable old-fashioned Pullmans, their cozy club cars, and their traditional dining cars. There were sound reasons for this reluctance. The Pennsylvania, based in the City of Brotherly Love, was, in the words of the premier railroad historian Lucius Beebe, "the best gentleman's club in Philadelphia." From its High Victorian–style Broad Street Station ran the "Clockers" between Philadelphia and New York, so-called because they departed their respective terminals on the hour. All carried the "Club" series of parlor-buffet cars, designed to make passengers forget that they had ever left Rittenhouse Square. Of course the nearest they got to Manhattan before the opening of Pennsylvania Station in 1916 was Jersey City, New Jersey, from where the passengers were ferried

ABOVE TOP The breakfast offerings on the *Queen Mary* included such things as kippered herring and salt mackerel, which puzzled not a few Americans. (Private Collection.)

ABOVE BOTTOM *Taming of the Horse*, gold lacquer panel by Jean Dunand, c.1935. This is a reduction by Dunand of one of his four 20-square-foot panels which decorated the smoking room of the *Normandie*. (Courtesy Maison Gerard, Ltd.)

LEFT Two of the glories of the Italian Line were the *Conte di Savoia* and the *Rex* of 1932. In August 1933, the *Rex*, Mussolini's bold challenge to the new ships of other nations, captured the Blue Riband for crossing the Atlantic in 4 days, 13 hours, 58 minutes. (Private Collection.)

across the Hudson to West Street. The Vanderbilts' New York Central still jealously held the key to Manhattan rail service.

And no wonder, for the Pennsylvania had a cutthroat rivalry with the Central, especially for the prestigious, highly lucrative New York–Chicago run. Its *Broadway Limited,* inaugurated in 1902, offered an "amanuensis" to take dictation from the brokers and bankers aboard, immediate market reports, and expensive engraved stationery, a few sheets of which the passenger was expected to take away. The *Broadway*'s mahogany-paneled dining room with stewards in dinner jackets at night and striped morning trousers at breakfast revealed that the directors of the line had a view of the correct décor for modern transportation that was remarkably similar to the one that had led Cunard and White Star to float the drawing rooms of England out upon the sea. It was a point of view shared by the New York Central, whose brilliantly named *Twentieth Century Limited*, also inaugurated in 1902, was replete with bottle glass in its dining car windows and rich velour upholstery in its club cars.

Just as the First World War would be a watershed for the ocean liner, hard economic realities would pave the way for Art Deco trains and the handiwork upon the rails of two supreme industrial designers, Raymond Loewy and Henry Dreyfuss. The economic reality was the Great Depression of the 1930s and the proliferation of the private automobile. Both drained passengers from the railroads. Design was seen as a dramatic way to make rail travel once again modern. The theoretical reality behind the new configuration was "aerodynamics," a term succinctly defined by the industrial designer Norman Bel Geddes in his 1932 book, *Horizons*: "The subject of aerodynamics is anything but simple. Some applications of its principles, however, are not difficult to define. An object is streamlined when its exterior surface is so designed that upon passing through a fluid such as water or air the object creates the least disturbance."

The first American streamliners, which would have an impact on the Pennsylvania and New York Central, began their lives far from Gotham. The palm for being first must go to the Union Pacific's M-10000 — "M" for motor-powered — delivered by the Pullman Company of Chicago in February of 1934. Drawing upon futuristic design, the one-Pullman, two-coach train with its yellow and brown aluminum cars and distinctive snub-nosed gas-powered engine drew wondering crowds on a cross-country tour. Among the train's more than one million visitors was President Franklin D. Roosevelt, who perceived the M-10000 as a symbol of the progressive spirit he wished to bring to America. The power of modern design to appeal to potential passengers, as proven by the popularity of the M-10000, led the Burlington to introduce later in 1934 the amazing silver-colored *Zephyr*. Its slant front engine designed by Albert Dean working with the builder, the Budd Company, could zip along at an astounding 100 miles an hour. The interiors of the Union Pacific's train had been run-of-the-mill. For the *Zephyr*'s interiors Burlington turned to Paul Philippe Cret, the head of the School of Architecture at the University of Pennsylvania whose Hall of Science at Chicago's 1933 Century of Progress exhibition had garnered accolades. Cret's lounge observation car, with its curved glassed-in viewing area, its touches of chrome, and its blue

ABOVE The 1934 Burlington *Zephyr*, with its diesel engine and stainless steel construction was a pioneer in streamlined design. At 109 miles per hour, it covered the 1,015 miles between Denver and Chicago in 13 hours and 5 minutes. (Private Collection.)

RIGHT One of the supreme Art Deco railway posters was created by Andre Mouran, who signed himself "Cassandre," for the British Railway Company of F. McCorquodale & Co. The French artist has used the engine's wheels to convey a vibrant sense of power and speed, just as Henry Dreyfuss did with the unsheathed wheels of the engines pulling the *Twentieth Century Limited*. (Private Collection.)

upholstered metal chairs, was one of the first Art Deco train interiors. It was also Cret, who, confronted with the problem of strengthening the train's thin, stainless steel exterior, turned for a model to Thomas Jefferson's one-brick-thick garden walls at the University of Virginia. Noting that Jefferson had given his walls stability and strength by designing them in a curved, serpentine form, Cret fluted the exteriors of the *Zephyr*. Thus, fortuitously, utility and a modern material were united in a form which perfectly expressed movement.

With the appearance of trains like the *Zephyr* and in 1937 the *Super Chief*, also designed by Cret, which linked Chicago to Los Angeles, the Pennsylvania and the New York Central were forced to act. Passengers could not fail to notice the difference between the Deco trains which whisked them from the Windy City to the Pacific and the stale Gilded Age grandeur of those which carried them to the Atlantic. "It's a step backward in time to leave the *Chief* and board the *Twentieth Century*," a *Chicago Tribune* reporter observed. It was this urgent necessity to place in service trains which did not look hopelessly outdated which would lead to a rare *entente cordiale* between the Pennsylvania and the New York Central. In 1936 the Central had commissioned Henry Dreyfuss to update its *Mercury* for the profitable Detroit-Cleveland run. The success of the new *Mercury*'s soft, indirect lighting, pastel colors, and comfortable Art Deco–style lounge chairs led the line to ask Dreyfuss to transform the *Twentieth Century Limited*. When Philadelphia heard what was about to happen in New York, the fear of the effect that an all-new Century would have on its *Broadway Limited* led to an unprecedented proposal. In order to cut costs, both lines would streamline their two deluxe trains as a joint effort, and introduce them on the same day. The New York Central agreed. It was a brilliant headline-catching move and an economically sound one, for both trains were to be built by Pullman and thus, as far as basic construction and engineering were concerned, both were identical. The difference would come in their Art Deco décor, created by Loewy and Dreyfuss.

Born in France in 1893, Raymond Loewy was educated at the École de Lanneau, a school noted for its technical training, and at the University of Paris. After serving in the French army in the First World War, he emigrated to the United States in 1919 and settled in New York City. Loewy quickly made a name for himself in the worlds of fashion illustration and advertising, working for, among others, Wanamaker's, Saks Fifth Avenue, and Bonwit Teller. But he was always fascinated by industrial design and carved a niche for himself modernizing the Gestetner Duplicator, suggesting up-to-date coachwork for Detroit's Hupp Motor Company, and creating the modern, popular Coldspot refrigerator for Sears, Roebuck. In 1937 Loewy was asked by the Pennsylvania Railroad to give its new 6,000-horsepower electric locomotive a contemporary look. His envelope of welded smooth metal, the quintessence of streamlined design, which encased the powerful engine, caused a sensation. In time, Loewy gave a new look to almost every aspect of the Pennsy, from trashcans to timetables, from menus to toothpick wrappers.

Loewy's redesigned *Broadway Limited* was the flagship of what the Pennsy proclaimed "A Fleet of Modernism." Now utility, the driving power of the GG-1 series of electric locomotives which carried the train to the end of its electrified line at Harrisburg, Pennsylvania, and its magnificent

Pacific-type steam locomotives which pulled it on to Chicago, would be given an enveloping sheath of streamlined contours and painted a Tuscan red highlighted with gold stripes which swept back in a vivid "V" from its nose to make manifest the excitement of speed. The *Broadway*'s new lightweight cars were also Tuscan red with maroon bands linking their windows and with the same golden speed lines racing down their sides. Within, all recollections of horsehair and dark paneling were banished. In a quintessentially Deco manner Loewy employed unusual materials, light wood veneers, engraved glass, metal stripes, cork, and unexpected colors such as red and yellow with touches of black. In a daring and sometimes criticized innovation, Loewy replaced windows with walls decorated by murals, in both dining and lounge areas. The motivation behind this revolutionary concept was that whereas the trains of the New York Central began their journey westward with the breathtaking panorama of the Hudson unfolding before the passengers, the Pennsylvania could offer only the industrial wasteland of New Jersey. Loewy argued that the murals and the faces of other passengers sipping martinis and old-fashioneds were highly preferable to the chimney stacks and gasworks of Bayonne and Elizabeth.

If the *Normandie* possessed an ineffable glamour which transcended that of any other ship, so the *Twentieth Century Limited* outclassed all other trains. From its inception in 1902 the all-Pullman pride of the Vanderbilts regularly carried on its 20-hour overnight run between America's two greatest cities an impressive freight of financiers, actors, and socialites. So alluring was the *Century* that journalist-wit H. L. Mencken quipped that Chicago had only two things New York did not: "The Pompeiian Room in the Congress Hotel and the *Twentieth Century* back to New York." The difference between the *Twentieth Century* of the teens, twenties, and early thirties and the train after 1938 was the difference between superb rail transportation and the seamless melding of modern locomotive power and comfort with marvelous Art Deco design. The genius behind this creation was Henry Dreyfuss. Born in Manhattan in 1904, Dreyfuss attended the Ethical Culture Society's Arts High School, where he received invaluable instruction in both art history and in the actual techniques employed by artists. Afterwards an Ethical Culture Society scholarship made it possible for him to study during the winter of 1922–23 with Norman Bel Geddes, who was teaching theatrical design in his studio. Dreyfuss was, in fact, to make a name for himself as a theatrical designer in the 1920s and early 1930s. Among his credits were the sets for such hits as Jerome Kern's *The Cat and the Fiddle*. But like Geddes he quickly moved from the world of the theater into that of industrial design where his amazing talents transformed the look of Bell telephones, Hoover vacuum cleaners, and Big Ben alarm clocks.

Dreyfuss began work on the *Century* in 1936, and his designs for the Central's powerful Hudson locomotives, which pulled the train west from Harmon, New York, quickly became Art Deco icons. Like a silver spaceship, with its bold fin curving around its front and over its back, the engine appeared to slide through the air. And while the wheels of the Pennsylvania's locomotives were shrouded by Loewy's streamlined sheath, Dreyfuss boldly decided to leave the Central's engine's wheels and rods fully exposed in order to exhibit the mechanical power which drove the

Dreyfuss's dining car on the 1938 *Twentieth Century Limited* allowed passengers like Noël Coward, Beatrice Lillie, and Cole Porter to sip martinis and dine on filet mignon during the 16-hour run between Gotham and the Windy City in a brittle Deco setting. (Private Collection.)

train at 60 to 80 miles an hour. The futuristic quality of the engine was reiterated by the palette of the *Century*'s cars, silver, with touches of blue in their speed stripes, which gave the train a striking metallic modernity. Those who stepped aboard the new *Twentieth Century* at Grand Central on its inaugural run on June 15, 1938, were in for an aesthetic revelation. There were no longer any old-fashioned Pullmans with upper and lower berths, but only rooms on this, America's first all-room train. The dining cars of the *Century* were indisputable triumphs of Deco design comparable to the latest chic *boîtes* in Paris and New York. In order to banish as far as possible the sense of a corridor, Dreyfuss employed low glass walls at either end of the cars to create small dining areas for eight, while in the car's main body he used banquettes and tables of various sizes to avoid decorative monotony. Mirrors between the windows, Venetian blinds—the *dernier cri* of Deco modernity—and dramatic pipe lighting combined with sharply focused incandescent spots imbued the dining cars with an elegant, brittle 1930s style. Everything, from the napery to the matchbooks, to the china and the silver flatware, was designed by Dreyfuss and all bore the words "20th Century Limited," atop a logo consisting of a column of speed lines.

The redesigned *Century* was an immediate and unqualified success. While the *Broadway Limited* still seemed to carry with it more than a little of the fuddy-duddy atmosphere of Quaker Philadelphia, the *Century* evinced the brashness and the sophistication of New York. And the train always seemed to have good luck. When Ben Hecht and Charles MacArthur's 1934 film *Twentieth Century*, starring John Barrymore and Carole Lombard, was a blockbuster, the Pennsylvania helped finance a Hal Roach film, titled, not surprisingly, *Broadway Limited*. The film could no more match *Twentieth Century* than the Pennsylvania's train could match the Central's. After 1938 ridership on the *Broadway Limited* actually declined, while the *Twentieth Century*, in order to accommodate the demand for tickets, had to regularly run two or more sections.

In his immensely influential book *Vers une Architecture*, published in 1923, Le Corbusier charged his fellow architects to design their buildings in a manner which would reflect modern life as exemplified by, among other things, the automobile. Corbusier reemphasized this point in the 1931 documentary film *L'Architecture d'Aujourd'hui*, in which he famously showed his avant-garde Villa Savoye outside Paris, dubbing it "a machine for living" and related it to a shot of an automobile, "a machine for driving." This mode of conveyance, which was to profoundly change American society, was slow to embrace designs which expressed its essence—movement and speed. There is a curious dichotomy in the alluring automobile advertisements of the 1920s and early 1930s. While the slender, bobbed-hair young women and handsome, athletic young men getting in or out of or speeding along in their Buicks, Cadillacs, Packards, Fords, and Hupmobiles radiate modernity, the high, boxy, carriage-like automobiles themselves seem more appropriate for a Boston dowager than for a red-blooded, up-to-date American girl. One answer to this puzzle was provided by Norman Bel Geddes in *Horizons*: "One of the chief factors restraining the manufacturer from making more fundamental annual changes in his cars is the cost of tooling up and the cost of dies. To make a complete set of dies for a motor car requires a considerable expenditure of money. The present method is to alter annually as few dies as possible, sufficient however to make changes which will be noticed by the public, and which may be advertised as the new model."

A few automobile designers, though, were attempting to craft a vehicle which would both aesthetically express its reality and facilitate its movement. In the 1920s, Errett Lobban Cord, at his Auburn Automobile Company, lowered the center of gravity of his cars and made their design more aerodynamic. In the same decade Glenn Curtiss, a pioneering aviation designer, conducted a number of sensational experiments proving that through streamlining, the speed of the typical automobile could be increased by 20 percent when going 25 miles an hour. Two American automakers did fully embrace this concept. The Pierce-Arrow Company, in 1933, introduced five handmade prototypes of

Even when the automobiles themselves were not streamlined, manufacturers tried to make them appear so in advertisements. Interestingly, while the woman in this 1927 Hupmobile ad embodies modern style, the car she is helping sell is a boxy horseless carriage. (Private Collection.)

their beautiful streamlined *Silver Arrow,* which, with its sweeping fenders and fastback, finally brought Deco design to the American highway. Alas, neither Pierce-Arrow nor its parent company, Studebaker, could afford to put the *Silver Arrow* into production and Pierce-Arrow itself would disappear in 1938. Chrysler, though, with its 1934–37 Chryslers and DeSotos, did bring to the mass market its new streamlined "Airflow" designs. While the cars handled well and were exceedingly comfortable, their ungainly exteriors were universally ridiculed. They were, in the words of one critic, of a "rhinocerine ungainliness."

There was no ungainliness about the Special Coupe produced by Germany's Mercedes-Benz, whose founders, Carl Benz and Gottlieb Daimler, had, in 1886, introduced the internal combustion engine to the world. With their Model S of 1927—its center of gravity lowered, its fenders dramatically swept back—the firm moved toward true streamlining. This was given brilliant form in their 1936 Special Coupe 540K. Manufactured in the firm's Sindelfingen plant, the 540 K was the culmination of the work of German, British, and French coach builders. Here at last was a true aerodynamic design where fenders flowing back to the rear wheels and a daringly slanted windshield, dashing touches of chrome, and parabolic side windows combined to express drop-dead Deco smartness. Intended to make a splash at the 1936 Berlin auto show, the Coupe did just that. After the 540K, automobile makers in both Europe and America knew that, whatever the cost, the era of modern design had arrived.

While it took decades for the automobile to embrace modernity, that was never the scenario with the airplane, for the airplane was essentially a combination of dual design necessities

ABOVE The new Chrysler Straight Eights of 1930 showed that automakers were beginning to take seriously the design possibilities of aerodynamics. (Private Collection.)

RIGHT Art Deco's fascination with images of speed is exemplified by this advertisement. (Private Collection.)

OPPOSITE The George Washington Bridge was built to handle the enormous increase in automobile traffic coming into New York. The auto ownership in Bergen County, New Jersey, for example, increased 172 percent between 1923 and 1928 and studies showed that the capacity of ferries to carry them across the Hudson River was reaching its limits. Even in the first full year of the Great Depression, 1930–31, automobile traffic from New Jersey to New York went up 25 percent. When it opened in 1931 the 3,500-foot George Washington set a new record for length and doubled the existing suspension bridge record. The engineer responsible for this astonishing structure was Othmar Ammann of Switzerland. Originally its twin towers were to have a granite cladding designed by Cass Gilbert. But rising costs and a faltering economy led to their steel skeleton being left uncovered, thus producing one of the city's most impressive sights, two high towers whose cubistic forms fit perfectly into the Deco era. (Private Collection.)

mandated by the laws of physics. The plane's wings had to be airfoiled in order to produce the dynamic reaction which gave them lift, and the plane's body had to be streamlined to pass through the air with the least disturbance. Thus the airplane designer always had a single view in mind, which fit perfectly into the Deco canon. The airplane smoothly moved from Wilbur and Orville Wright's kitelike flying machine of 1903, through the armed biplane of the First World War, to the Goliath-Farman passenger liner of the early 1920s with its extravagant Art Deco upholstery, to Claude Dornier's six-propeller DO-X of 1929 which carried more than 150 passengers in its cabin and whose porthole-lined prow resembled a futuristic yacht.

By 1930 the General Motors affiliate, Fokker, was building airplanes whose roomy cabins sported Art Deco lighting fixtures, club chairs which would not have been out of place on the *Ile de France*, and upholstery and wall coverings in dynamic patterns depicting, appropriately, the constellations. In 1934 Douglas's DC-2, a snappy silver streamliner, began flying nonstop from Chicago to Newark, New Jersey. That the planes went only as far as Newark was not lost on New York's ever-vigilant Mayor Fiorello LaGuardia, who, when the airliner landed in New Jersey,

Among the best-known images of Art Deco modernity in the 1930s was the Greyhound bus. Here one of the company's beautifully streamlined 1937 Yellow Super Coaches made by General Motors gets a bath. (Photograph by Esther Bubley. Standard Oil Company of New Jersey Collection, Eckstrom Library, University of Louisville.).

refused to disembark. "I bought a ticket to New York and this is not New York," he declared. As August Hecksher recalled in *When Laguardia Was Mayor: New York's Legendary Years*: "After he had been photographed sitting stolidly in his seat in an otherwise empty plane, a rotund and defiant figure, the airline in desperation had flown him to Floyd Bennett Field." New York's first airport took shape the next year at North Beach in Queens. It was eventually named, appropriately, "La Guardia." The Little Flower understood, even in a time when ocean liners still plied the Hudson and trains by the hundreds swept into Pennsylvania Station and Grand Central Terminal, that there would come a day when New York would not be New York if passengers arriving by air thought that Newark was New York.

RIGHT A stylish personification of the modernity of flight was presented by the Airlines Terminal Building (lower left) on 42nd Street opposite Grand Central Terminal. Completed in 1940 from designs by John B. Peterkin, the handsome Art Deco edifice was embellished by two eagles by René Chambellan atop it and Otto Bach's stainless steel map of the world above the entrance. The facility handled reservations, ticketing, and luggage transfers for five airlines. It was also the center for limousine service to LaGuardia and other airports. In 1982 the Philip Morris Headquarters was constructed on the site of the demolished Airlines Terminal Building.(Private Collection.)

OPPOSITE TOP The alluring romance of the predominately white Pan American Clippers which winged to Cuba, South America, and finally to Europe is evident in this 1938 advertisement of one of the very moderne craft above New York. (Private Collection.)

OPPOSITE BOTTOM Passengers headed to Europe went through Delano & Aldrich's superb Art Deco Marine Terminal of 1939-40. A Deco eagle perches high atop the entrance to emphatically proclaim the structure's purpose. (Private Collection.)

# THE NEW HOTELS

"I moved into the Waldorf-Astoria towers, the year it opened, 1931, just after the debut of the depression," party-giver par excellence Elsa Maxwell wrote in her hilarious essay "Hotel Pilgrim," which appeared in *The Unofficial Palace of New York: A Tribute to the Waldorf-Astoria*, a 1939 collection of essays edited by Frank Crowninshield. "The Waldorf-Astoria," Elsa reported," had packed up its prewar antimacassars, its gilt chairs and lace curtains, its Peacock Alley and red plush portieres, and had moved up to 50th Street and Park Avenue. Its towers glistened high in the skies, whitely, like a twentieth-century Taj Mahal." Miss Maxwell soon felt quite at home in her 41st floor aerie, and, she recalled, the management was remarkably understanding when "I felt a party coming on."

The Waldorf management even permitted her to pitch her amazing "Barnyard Party" amid the tasteful green marble precincts of the Jade Room. The centerpiece of that bash was a life-sized cow—artificial of course—which squirted champagne from one teat and Scotch from another. To augment the Appalachian atmosphere, the hostess conjured up an apple orchard, with real apples tied to the trees and had, much to the dismay of a number of Upper East Side grande dames, live chickens, ducks, and pigs scurrying about under foot. A final fillip was a "hillbilly" band, which provided music for the square dancing led by a passel of New York socialites.

THIS PAGE The Waldorf-Astoria Hotel, Henry J. Hardenbergh's immense 1,300-room hotel which occupied the block on Fifth Avenue between 33rd and 34th streets, was actually two hotels, the Waldorf, completed in 1893, and the Astoria, which opened in 1897. In this 1898 view, looking south, the A. T. Stewart mansion rises just across 34th Street from the hotel, while the impressive brick building with awnings is the New-York Club. The Waldorf-Astoria was demolished in 1929 to make way for the Empire State Building. (Library of Congress.)

OPPOSITE The end of Prohibition led New York's hotels to look for ways to cash in on the new dispensation which permitted the public sale and consumption of alcohol. The Plaza, whose once-elegant Rose Room to the left of the Fifth Avenue entrance had been converted during the drought into a Studebaker showroom, turned the space over to Joseph Urban for conversion into a nightclub. His Persian Room took its name from Lillian Palmedo's five murals depicting scenes from the *Rubaiyat* of Omar Khayyam. Urban died in 1933, a year before the room opened, and the decorative scheme was finished by Joseph Urban Associates. With its 27-foot bar, its glittering black glass piers, and its reflecting ceiling, the Persian Room was the perfect setting for the sophisticated piano playing of Eddy Duchin, the dancing of the De Marcos, and the Parisian-inspired singing of the chanteuse, Hildegard. (The New York Public Library.)

Among the guests was Elsa's bosom buddy, Cole Porter, and Bert Lahr, who brought Beatrice Lillie. "I have never, I believe, given a better party," the portly Elsa asserted, sounding not a little like Noël Coward.

The difference between the Waldorf-Astoria of 1931 and the grandiose Belle Epoque caravansary of the same name which it succeeded paralleled the difference between the faux Adam-style first class drawing room on the prewar *Aquitania* and the soigné modernity of the postwar *Ile de France*. The old Waldorf was New York's ultimate incarnation of the 19th-century palace hotel. The history of this type of hostelry begins, in Gotham, in 1836 with the Greek Revival 309-room Astor House on lower Broadway designed by Isaiah Rogers, but, fashionable New York, ever peripatetic, soon moved north and the next notable hotel was the Fifth Avenue of 1859 on Madison Square. This six-story Italianate marble palace, the work of William Washburn, boasted New York's first passenger elevator. Other palace-type hotels quickly followed: the Hoffman House, just to the north of the Fifth Avenue, and the Windsor, even farther uptown at Fifth Avenue and 49th Street. Sophisticated New Yorkers found these lodgings woefully lacking in urban gravitas. Robert A. M. Stern, in *New York 1900*, notes that in 1889 an editor of *The Real Estate Record and Guide* complained that the city lacked "a really great hotel" and that there was "nothing distinctive, nothing metropolitan" about the ones it possessed. This civic self-flagellation was undoubtedly spurred on by the sumptuous new hostelries which had risen in Paris, like the 700-room Grand Hotel on the boulevard des Capucines near the Opéra, and the Continental, on the rue de Castiglione; as well as those recently built in London, including the Charing Cross next to the railway station of that name and the 400-room Langham in Portland Place.

The self-flagellation abruptly ceased when, in 1893, the Waldorf opened its doors. Here at last were appropriate precincts where newly minted millionaires and Knickerbocker socialites could snack and snooze. Constructed by William Waldorf Astor on the site of his father's house at the northwest corner of Fifth Avenue and 33rd Street, the 13-story hotel literally put in the shade the next-door mansion of his detested Aunt Caroline Webster Schermerhorn, who had married his father's younger brother, William Backhouse Astor, Jr. Seeing the writing on the wall next to her, the recently widowed Caroline, who had earned her nephew's antipathy by styling herself "The" Mrs. Astor, moved up Fifth Avenue to 65th Street. In 1897 the 17-story Astoria rose on the site of the brownstone mansion where "The" Mrs. Astor had once corralled New York's "400." (Tradition has it that the sacred number was a reference to the fact that Mrs. Astor's ballroom held only 400 people. "If you go outside that number," Ward McAllister, the leading social arbiter of the period, announced, "you strike people who are either not at ease in a ballroom or make other people not at ease.") Thus the 1,300-room Waldorf-Astoria or "Hyphen," as old New Yorkers always called it, was born. Both hotels were designed by Henry J. Hardenbergh in an eclectic mélange of styles which drew upon elements of the German and the Italian Renaissance with a bit of French Beaux Arts panache thrown in for good measure. The opulent hotel's Flemish-style café and Italian-style dining room, its 18th-century century French-inspired Astor Gallery and amber, marble-lined Peacock Alley stretching from 33rd to 34th streets, vouchsafed to New Yorkers the right to proclaim that they now possessed an inn that equaled any to be found in Paris or London. The novelist Henry James, a native-born New Yorker, had only praise for the edifice. It was for him "a gorgeous golden blur, a paradise, peopled with unmistakable American shapes."

By the end of the 1920s the plethora of architectural styles which had once drawn the upper crust to the Waldorf seemed as passé as one of those gilded Baroque dining rooms that Johannes Poppe had whipped up for 19th-century German ocean liners. Short-skirted shebas and young sheiks attired in the new tailless dinner jackets were not tempted to Charleston in a ballroom where, in the winter of 1897, the Bradley-Martins had thrown a Versailles-inspired costume ball at which the dance of choice had been the minuet.

The Waldorf-Astoria was kept afloat by a remarkable impresario, Lucius Boomer, who took over the helm in 1918 after Coleman Du Pont of the Delaware Du Ponts told him, "Boomer, I'll buy the Waldorf, if you'll run it." Du Pont knew exactly what he was getting in his new manager, for Lucius Boomer, when it came to running hotels, was a magician. A native of Poughkeepsie, New York, he had begun his hotel career working for Henry Flagler in Florida in the 1890s and had eventually moved on to managing the new McAlpine on Herald Square just west of the Waldorf. After he and Du Pont formed the Boomer–Du Pont Properties Corporation, they would acquire, along with other notable hotels, the Bellevue-Stratford in Philadelphia and the Willard in Washington, D.C., as well as the renowned Sherry's restaurant and catering business in New York.

But even Lucius Boomer's managerial magic wand could not prevent the carriage trade, upon whom the Waldorf depended, from flowing away up Fifth Avenue. Though B. Altman, like a self-assured dowager, remained catty-cornered from the hotel at the northeast corner of Fifth Avenue and 34th Street, many of the city's luxury retail establishments were now far north of 34th Street. There were already persistent rumors that Tiffany & Co. would abandon the ravishing palazzo Stanford White had designed for it at 37th Street and join in the trek up the Avenue. (Tiffany's would not make the leap northward until 1940.)

There was another critical matter, one facing not only the Waldorf-Astoria but every respectable hotel in the city. The passage of the Volstead Act—which went into effect in 1920— prohibiting the sale of any beverage containing more than one half of one percent alcohol siphoned off the customers who had once crowded the Waldorf's famed four-sided bar and its popular oak-paneled Men's Café. "Watering holes," one frequenter of the bar quipped, "have become deserts." Boomer devised dozens of stratagems to keep the cash flowing, including introducing a candy shop serving ice cream sodas and turning part of the fashionable Rose Room into a locale for afternoon tea. But though these enterprises were successful, the revenue they generated was but a drop in the bucket compared to that supplied by the sale of Scotch, gin, and champagne. And Prohibition also affected the hotel's important ballroom and dining room business. "People simply will not eat out if they are unable to get a drink," Boomer told the *New*

*York Times.* And then he added, "Fortunes are being made along Broadway by establishments which have little or no responsibility. We are being penalized for obeying the law." But necessity is indeed sometimes the mother of invention and now the wizard came up with a solution to deal with the constraints of prohibition that was at once brilliant and subtle: the apartment hotel.

Such an establishment would provide the tenant with an elegant, beautifully furnished suite of rooms and a service pantry. The hotel would, through its room service, provide meals of the highest quality, while the guest would supply his own wines and spirits—readily available in New York throughout Prohibition—with the hotel having absolutely no legal liability. The concept was tried out in the Boomer–Du Pont–owned Sherry-Netherland of 1927 at Fifth Avenue and 59th Street. It would have its supreme incarnation in the Tower suites of the new Waldorf-Astoria. In late December of 1928, the Boomer–Du Pont Properties Corporation sold their interest in the Waldorf-Astoria for $13,500,000. The site was to be used for a stupendous new office building, the Empire State. In recognition of all that he had done for the hotel, the board of directors, for one dollar, gave Boomer the rights to the name. Beginning May 1, 1929, the hotel's furnishings were sold and then New York's first true palace hotel was turned over to the wreckers.

Lucius Boomer's extraordinary talent for running hotels and creating the correct ambience to mesh with the taste of the times was about to have its greatest challenge and its greatest success. He and his wife, Jorgine, had just begun a two-week vacation in Florida, when a telegram arrived

from L. J. Horowitz, chairman of the board of Thompson-Starrett, one of New York's top builders. The company wanted a new Waldorf-Astoria. The telegram dramatically recalled the words that Senator Coleman Du Pont had spoken to Boomer in 1918. It read: "If you'll run it, I'll build it." And he would be, not a mere manager, but president.

On October 29, 1929—four months after Boomer began discussions about the new hotel—the stock market, in the immortal words of *Variety*, "Laid an egg." Or, as the writer Donald Ogden Stewart put it: "Everybody that afternoon had lost every shirt he had." With the joke making the rounds that when a broker or banker requested a room on a high floor in a New York or Chicago hotel, the desk clerk would routinely inquire, "Do you want it to sleep or leap?" this scarcely seemed an opportune time to construct a deluxe hotel. But the financing for the new Waldorf was already in place and it was considered less risky to proceed than to face the legal penalties which would result from not carrying out the corporation's obligations. Distinguished investment firms like Hayden, Stone & Company had agreed to underwrite the project, the New York Central, alongside of whose tracks the hotel would be situated, had pledged 10 million dollars, the contracts for furnishings had been signed, and the builder's schedule drawn up. The entire package— including the cost of the site—came to an impressive 40 million dollars.

The colossal hotel which rose on Park Avenue between 49th and 50th streets, a site previously occupied by the New York Central's powerhouse and the Railroad Branch of the YMCA, exemplified the melding of European Art Deco design and American vertical modernity. The Waldorf's cubistic volumes, wonderfully expressed in its 18-story Park Avenue façade and in its 47-story main section, which the architects Leonard Schultz and Lloyd Morgan of Schultz & Weaver brilliantly pivoted at right angles to Park Avenue, clearly draw upon Art Deco sources. So too do the hotel's twin metal-capped turrets, which suggest the fantasy drawings of the Italian Futurist Antonio Sant'Elia. But the fundamental form of the hotel is unabashedly American. Forty years earlier, the renowned Chicago architect Louis Sullivan, in his essay "The Tall Office Building Artistically Considered," had declared that the essential aesthetic of the tall building was its very tallness and that the new urban tower must be "a proud and a soaring thing." Now, in the assertive verticality of the Waldorf's grey granite, limestone, and brick walls mounting 625 feet into the air, Sullivan's words were made manifest. But on Park Avenue it was not an office building that gave life to his dicta, but that most American of all building types, the residential skyscraper. The only other hotel of comparative modernity was the Dorchester in London's Park Lane, completed the same year as the Waldorf. Designed by William Curtis Green, the Dorchester, with its graceful shallow curving façade, its skin of terrazzo panels, and its rhythmical cantilevered balconies, is an exquisite essay in English Deco architecture. But at just 10 stories, the Dorchester is inextricably tied to the European tradition of low-rise buildings; the Waldorf-Astoria, on the other hand, is brazenly New World, New York, boldly lifting its occupants into the sky.

The most striking impression of the interior of the Waldorf-Astoria is its longitudinality, for this is an ocean liner layout bringing to the asphalt and concrete of Park Avenue the aura of the

59989

Park Avenue Entrance

ABOVE *The Spirit of Achievement*, a quintessential Art Deco conception, crowns the Waldorf's Park Avenue entrance. The cast nickel-bronze statue is by Nina Saemundsson. (Historic Architecture Collection, The Art Institute of Chicago.)

LEFT The Waldorf's 18-story Park Avenue façade, the creation of Lloyd Morgan of Schultz & Weaver, is an impeccable example of Deco urbanism. The architect has opted for a simplified Modern Classical style, with the decorative touches provided by the tall metal grilles above the entrances and the bas-reliefs by Charles Keck flanking the hotel's name. (Historic Architecture Collection, The Art Institute of Chicago.)

BOTTOM  The main foyer looking eastward toward
the lobby. The tall Art Deco gold and silver urns
contained lights. (Historic Architecture Collection,
The Art Institute of Chicago.)

TOP  The admirably restrained Art Deco Park
Avenue foyer of the Waldorf is enhanced with a
painted frieze by the French artist Louis Rigal, who
also designed the *Wheel of Life* rug—now replicat-
ed in mosaic— whose central medallion depicts the
drama of human life from cradle to grave. (The
Waldorf-Astoria Hotel.)

grand salons and dining rooms of the great French liners. This is an interior radically different from those of Belle Epoque hotels such as New York's Plaza, which is, like the earlier Waldorf-Astoria, the creation of Henry J. Hardenbergh. Whether entered from its Grand Army Plaza side to the east or its 59th Street side to the north, the Plaza Hotel presents to the visitor a series of grand architectural boxes, boxes more often than not accessible only by turning left or right and then proceeding down long corridors. Not so at the Waldorf.

Upon entering the Waldorf-Astoria from its Park Avenue side one ascends a broad flight of stairs—subtly reminiscent of a gangway—to the main foyer, a chamber, both by its location and décor, inescapably recalling the main embarkation halls or grand foyers of 1930s ocean liners. With its fluted piers and their diminutive gilded capitals, bisque-colored walls, and tall moderne silver and gold urns throwing light upon the silver-leaf ceiling, the room is a paean to the Art Deco style. Straight ahead, as on a liner, lies a vast, fully revealed space. Here, because this is a hotel, the space is not a dining room, but the Waldorf's stupendous 80-foot-long lobby. Now the palette dramatically mutates from the lightness of the main foyer to a dark splendor. This windowless chamber—another reference to the ocean liner—is adorned with black marble piers of an Egyptian cast, their vestigial capitals gilded, and Deco-style boiseries consisting of broad swaths of ebony and Oregon maple embellished with bands of bronze and nickel. The lobby's ceiling, in its use of materials both exotic and contemporary—bronze, nickel, imitation ivory—echoes the work of French *ébénistes* like Émile-Jacques Ruhlmann. (The term *ébéniste*

ABOVE For its ballroom, the Waldorf-Astoria used a small-scale version of F. Schumacher & Co.'s rayon damask *Les Gazelles au Bois*, which the company had introduced in 1927. The design was inspired by a wrought-iron fire screen by Edgar Brandt. (F. Schumacher & Co.)

BELOW LEFT The Waldorf's Sert Room, to the left of the Park Avenue entrance, took its name from the 15 murals in brown and silver tones by the distinguished Spanish painter, José María Sert. The murals depicted scenes from Cervantes's *Don Quixote*. The sophisticated space was a favorite rendezvous for New York socialites and business leaders for luncheon, dinner, and after-dinner dancing. (Library of Congress.)

An important element of Art Deco architecture, an element that makes it so appealing, is that it often gave steel and concrete expression to the celluloid fantasies of the 1920s and 1930s. The Waldorf-Astoria is a conspicuous example. Its twin-towered exterior embodied, aesthetically, aspects of the futurist city in Fritz Lang's memorable 1927 film *Metropolis* (opposite), while the atmosphere of its luxurious lobby captured the ambience of MGM's *Grand Hotel* (above). (Private Collection.)

originally referred to a master cabinetmaker who worked in *bois d'ébène* (ebony) and other precious woods; later, it was more generally applied to any maker of luxury furniture.) All of the lobby's furniture was contemporary, of light walnut banded with metal and upholstered in green and beige leather. It could have been borrowed from the *Ile de France.* Beyond the lobby is the elevator foyer, placed again as it would be on a ship, where elevators whisk guests to the grand ballroom on the third floor, decorated with Schumacher's rayon damask fabric with its moderne pattern of leaping deer among stylized flora, *Les Gazelles au Bois.* By the time the visitor descends the stairway leading to Lexington Avenue on the Waldorf's eastern side, he has traversed an uninterrupted interior space of a stupendous 405 feet.

An impressive galaxy of talent was assembled to craft the Waldorf's interiors, including New York's W. & J. Sloane, L. Alvoine et Cie of Paris, successor firm to Allard et Fils, which had created the interiors of a number of Newport's most magnificent "cottages," and White, Allom & Co. of London, who designed the interiors of the principal rooms in New York's Frick mansion. Lucius Boomer, whom Elsa Maxwell rightly characterized as the hotel's "presiding genius," was the force behind the drive for design perfection. And Boomer must be given credit for the modernity of the Waldorf's lobby and some of its other public rooms. While the hotel was under construction, Boomer and his Swedish-born wife toured Europe, studying, among other things, Scandinavian modern design, including Stockholm's just-completed City Hall. As a result of this trip, Nordiska Kompaniet of Stockholm, one of Sweden's leading decorators, fabricated an unabashedly modern suite for the Waldorf. Boomer's somewhat surprising receptivity to modern design is explained in part by the comments of a friend: "Every new style interested him, for he realized that a hotel to succeed must reflect changing taste. He studied the 1925 Paris Exposition like a textbook."

Another, not to be underestimated, factor helping to push modernity into the Waldorf was film. Though a number of 1920s French films had Art Deco sets and the great German director Fritz Lang had depicted a Deco city of the future in *Metropolis* of 1927, it was Cedric Gibbons who brought the Art Deco style home to American filmgoers. Gibbons would be the first American to emblazon on the silver screen the proposition that to be chic, sophisticated, and truly contemporary one had to dwell in moderne houses, dance in moderne nightclubs, and patronize moderne hotels. Born in Dublin in 1893, the son and grandson of architects, Gibbons studied at New York's Art Students League and became a draftsman in his father's office, but he abandoned Gotham for Hollywood after the First World War. There he led a fabled life, designing the Oscar statuette, marrying the beauteous Dolores Del Rio, and residing in a house in Santa Monica so up-to-date that it could have been a set for one of his movies. After 1925, Gibbons persuaded Louis B. Mayer to discard the painted backdrops and Jacobean and Spanish Revival furniture in his films and to begin building three-dimensional sets with furnishings reflecting the latest Paris designs.

In 1928 Gibbons and the exceptional artistic staff he assembled produced what is arguably Hollywood's first film with all-modern sets, *Our Dancing Daughters,* starring Joan Crawford. Here, in the words of Howard Mandelbaum and Eric Myers in *Screen Deco*, Gibbons "unveiled the spacious Art Deco style for which he became famous." Indeed the film audaciously brought to the screen the design aesthetics of the 1925 Paris Exposition which Gibbons had visited time and again. And he was the supervisory art director for the visually sensational *Grand Hotel,* which was released in 1932, the year after the Waldorf opened for business. In this mythic Berlin hostelry, whose lobby is a series of dynamic circles, a weary Russian ballerina (Greta Garbo), an impoverished German baron (John Barrymore), a desperate capitalist (Wallace Beery), a dying bookkeeper (Lionel Barrymore), and an opportunistic stenographer (Joan Crawford) participate in a dramatic ronde, spinning through life as though on a speeding carousel. Viewing the film in the movie palaces of America, audiences in Keokuk, Kankakee, and Kenosha knew that, while Berlin's Grand Hotel was a cinematographic fantasy, in New York, on Park Avenue, there existed a concrete and steel hotel which, with its swank and chic, surpassed even the Grand.

While *Grand Hotel* may have been the most memorable Art Deco celluloid hotel, numerous other 1930s films used Deco hotels to convey a sense of stylish glamour. In the first film in which they costarred, RKO's *The Gay Divorcee* of 1934, Fred Astaire and Ginger Rogers were incandescent dancing "The Continental" in the open courtyard of an English seaside hotel. Not a little of the incandescence, though, emanated from the resort's sparking silver and glass revolving doors, its high curved towers, and the circular patterned dance floor which combined to project spectacular Deco chic. And in Universal's 1936 screwball comedy *My Man Godfrey*, starring William Powell as a down-and-out Depression era "forgotten man" and Carole Lombard as a New York socialite, Lombard wins first prize at a scavenger hunt organized as a charity event for bringing Powell to the "Waldorf Ritz" hotel. With its bold chevron-patterned walls, Art Deco glass entrances, and streamlined bar, the "Waldorf Ritz" blatantly suggests the actual hostelry that was its prototype.

The Waldorf was not the only remarkable Art Deco–inspired hotel to rise in New York. There was the Carlyle on Madison Avenue of 1929, featuring furnished and unfurnished apartments designed by Bien & Prince; Sugarman & Berger's Hotel New Yorker on Eighth Avenue of 1930, a colossal Deco slab which proudly advertised that, because it had 92 telephone operators working its 41st-floor switchboard, guests never missed a call; and the streamlined 26-story Panhellenic by John Mead Howells on First Avenue whose original clientele consisted of women who were members of Greek letter sororities. But the Waldorf-Astoria, because of the quality of its design and its superb location, which allowed it to rise above the Byzantine dome of St. Bartholomew's Church like an artificial Matterhorn, was the undisputed jewel in the crown of Gotham's new hotels. Thus it is not surprising that when in the afternoon of September 30, 1931, the hotel was previewed by specially invited guests, no one less than President Herbert Hoover—by radio from the White House—addressed the throng assembled in the ballroom. "The erection of this great structure at this time," the President said, "has been a contribution to the maintenance of employment and an exhibition of courage and confidence to the whole nation."

Hoover proved that he did indeed believe the structure to be "great" by moving in after he turned over the White House to Franklin Delano Roosevelt in March of 1933. Hoover's suite was on the 40th floor, just below Cole Porter's. It is a testimony to the solidity of the Waldorf's construction—the hotel proudly advertised that its rooms were "soundproof"—that there is no record of the former president complaining of being disturbed by Porter composing, as was his wont, after midnight on one of his two grand pianos. If the hotel had not been quite so solid he might have heard these lines from "You're the Top," which graced Porter's 1934 hit, *Anything Goes:* "You're the top! You're an Arrow collar! You're the top! You're a Coolidge dollar!" The ex-President might possibly have noted that the composer had not declared, "You're a Hoover dollar!"

ABOVE The 46-story Hotel Carlyle of 1929 rises above the foliage of Central Park with the Bethesda Fountain in the foreground. The limestone and yellow brick tower, located on Madison Avenue between 76th and 77th streets, was designed by Bien & Prince. It is an outstanding example of Art Deco co-opting Byzantine and Romanesque architectural elements and transforming them into an urbane modernity. (Hotel Carlyle.)

LEFT The massive Art Deco Hotel New Yorker on 34th Street at 8th Avenue boasted that each of its 2,500 rooms had a radio. (Private Collection.)

RIGHT Another splendid example of Art Deco borrowing aspects of past styles and transforming them is evident in John Mead Howells's 22-story Panhellenic Tower (now Beekman Tower) of 1928 at the northeast corner of First Avenue and 49th Street. Howells, who with Raymond Hood designed the Gothic Revival *Chicago Tribune* tower, completed in 1925, used the unbroken upward sweep of his yellow brick piers to provide the same sense of verticality given to the *Tribune* tower by its flying buttresses. Though the Panhellenic is unreservedly modern in its design, there lingers about it a ghost of the Gothic. (Private Collection.)

OPPOSITE In 1929 Helmle, Corbett & Harrison completed a 27-story apartment hotel at One Fifth Avenue just north of Washington Square. In 1926 when the architects began the design process, the structure was a mass of Venetian details, but by the time it was completed, One Fifth's simplified cubistic massing made it an Art Deco campanile in Greenwich Village. (Private Collection.)

THE NEW HOTELS

# SHOPS AND SHOPPING À LA MODE

The photograph is of Paris in 1925. It is the key year to understanding Art Deco and to understanding the persona of the new woman of that year, for it is the year that L'Exposition Internationale des Arts Décoratifs et Industriels Modernes took place in Paris and the year that the revolutionary forces which had been shaping fashion since the Great War coalesced to produce Coco Chanel's "little black dress." The view is looking up the avenue de l'Opéra near the Théâtre Français.

Architecturally the avenue is virtually unchanged since Baron Haussmann began slicing it through old Paris for Emperor Napoleon III in the 1860s. Every building is essentially a classically inspired Beaux Arts composition of pilasters, string courses, conspicuous cornices, and because this is Paris, mansard roofs. But the women on the street bear no resemblance to the females of the Second Empire or even to the women of a mere decade earlier. Vanished are the large, wide-brimmed hats, vanished too the silhouette which emphasized certain aspects of the female figure, hips and busts, vanished, most noticeably of all, the long skirts which concealed legs down to the ankle. The same radical transformation of the female of the species was evident on Chicago's State Street, Boston's Beacon Street, and New York's Fifth Avenue.

The two events which had transmuted the woman of, say, 1915, into the woman of 1925 were the First World War and the 19th Amendment to the U. S. Constitution—signed into law on August 26, 1920—which gave women the right to vote. Beyond allowing women access to the

BELOW This view of Paris's avenue de l'Opéra in 1925 vividly illustrates the revolutionary change in women's dress which followed the First World War. (Roger-Viollet.)

OPPOSITE Ely Jacques Kahn's vibrant glazed terra-cotta decoration on the façade of 261 Fifth Avenue of 1928 gave an appropriate pizzazz to a structure housing the showrooms and offices of a number of important textile firms. The designs reflect the pursuit by Art Deco architects of inspiration outside the classical canon, or what Kahn called the "everlasting rewarming of New England." Instead, Kahn noted, "Are not Cambodia, China, Mexico, Tibet also our cultural heritage?" In this he was in agreement with Frank Lloyd Wright, who also rejected the decorative legacy of ancient Greece and Rome and often turned instead to the Far East and pre-Columbian America. Indeed at 261 Kahn's decorative program bears a marked similarity to elements of Wright's Barnsdall House of 1920 in Los Angeles. Kahn's decorations on the piers of 261 are, in fact, a blown-up version of the stylized hollyhocks on the Barnsdall residence. (Photograph by John Cadenhead.)

ballot, the advent of universal suffrage had a profound psychological concomitant. It made women feel that they were now truly equal to men as fellow human beings with entrée to every field of endeavor. The aspirations of pioneering suffragettes like Alva Vanderbilt Belmont, who had boldly led a "Votes for Women" parade down Fifth Avenue in 1912, were now realized. Alva had expressed some of those aspirations in a musical play she had written with Elsa Maxwell, *Melinda and Her Sisters*. Performed at the old Waldorf-Astoria Hotel on February 18, 1916, *Melinda* concluded with the song, "Girls, Girls!" the rousing refrain of which went like this:

> *Girls, Girls, put away your curls,*
> *Come, put away your petticoats and frills!*
> *Step right into line,*
> *Cease now to repine,*
> *We'll show them that we all can learn to drill.*
> *Left! Right!*

Though the order to march was intended to encourage women to quickstep for suffrage and perhaps to play a role in the European war even before the United States officially became a participant, in retrospect it had an even greater significance. For as men marched off to France in 1917, women took the opportunity to march into the jobs vacated by them. Suddenly females, who, if they did not marry, were expected to take up "respectable careers," such as teaching, nursing, social work or stenography, were moving into restaurant management, real estate, and interior decoration, and into fields which were stepping-stones to corporate power: department stores, fashion magazines, and cosmetics. Harry W. Yoxall, head of *Vogue*'s London office for 40 years, records, in his 1966 autobiography *A Fashion of Life,* the energy released by this feminist offensive:

> It is ridiculous to speak of women as the weaker sex in any but the physical sense. Often in business I've seen them display the most astounding audacity. I think of some of the American female tycoons, the dollar princesses of some of the fields I've touched, such as Helena Rubinstein [founder of the famed cosmetics firm], Dorothy Shaver [president of the Lord & Taylor department store], and Carmel Snow [editor of *Harper's Bazaar*]. They showed themselves far more ruthless than the most determined men I've known. Certainly they were many times more resourceful.

The mention of Helena Rubinstein—and one must add the name of Elizabeth Arden—brings up the matter of cosmetics. For their use was just as revolutionary a signal as was the creeping upward of the hemline. Consuelo Vanderbilt Balsan, the daughter of Alva Vanderbilt Belmont, in her 1925 recollections *The Glitter and the Gold*, relates the generally accepted rules before the First World War: "No well-bred woman could afford to look seductive, at least not in public. Lipstick and powder alone were considered fast, and any further embellishments would immediately have

During the 1920s John Held, Jr.'s drawings of life in the fast lane appeared in *Century Magazine*, *Vanity Fair*, *Harper's Bazaar*, *Redbook*, and the *New Yorker*. This quintessential Held was a 1925 cover for *Judge* magazine, a satirical revue that ran from 1881 well into the 1930s. The artist has depicted the "new woman" as a gay femme fatale with her short dress, rolled silk stockings, lipstick, and cloche. And there can be no doubt that she will welcome a swig from the proffered hip flask. (Culver Pictures, Inc.)

OPPOSITE PAGE, TOP RIGHT Katherine Hartford, in this 1929 Realsilk ad, personifies the new woman. (Private Collection.)

OPPOSITE PAGE, LEFT AND BOTTOM The hallmarks of the new woman were the sliplike "little black dress" and head-hugging cloche from Paris milliners like Camille Roger. (Private Collection.)

ABOVE Noted dress and hat designer, Suzanne Talbot, seen here in her Eileen Gray–decorated Paris apartment. (Thérèse Bonney/ Bibliothèque Historique de la Ville de Paris.)

LEFT In the 1920s and early 1930s cloches were worn by every fashion-conscious woman over a close-cropped head. Anita Loos, the author of Gentlemen Prefer Blondes, claimed to have been the first to bob her hair. (Private Collection.)

committed one to the world of the 'déclassé.'" The change in attitude after the war was dramatic. Just back from a stint with the Red Cross in France, the very proper Carmel Snow recalled that at *Vogue,* where she was then working, "We were beginning, now, to assist nature a trifle with our faces—a touch of Roger & Gallet lipstick, gardenia-white Hudnut powder, a circle of Doreen rouge." Neither the ladies at *Vogue* nor the shoppers at B. Altman's or Saks were discouraged from their desire "to assist nature" by the warning of Dorothy Speare in *Dancers in the Dark* that "the intoxication of rouge is an insidious vintage." By 1925 it was estimated that American women were shelling out millions of dollars a year to make themselves "seductive."

There is no doubt that there was a strong sexual element, a desire to please the American male returning from France, in both the new woman's use of lipstick, rouge, and powder and in her new raiment. Harry Yoxall, always a perceptive analyst, deals with the underlying motivation:

During all my time the debate has continued as to whether women dress for other women, or for men. . . . [I]n my observation its underlying motive is sexual. Its object is to win or hold a man. It is true that women dress to attract other women's attention or to rouse their envy; but the gauge of their success is their effect on men.

The doughboys who returned home from Europe in 1919 or 1920 were often very different beings from the ones who had sailed eastward in 1917 or 1918. There had been innumerable quick European marriages, prostitution was prevalent near the front and in the French capitol, and anyway the Mademoiselles from Armentières were usually willing. In Paris the young Americans had seen quite respectable women wearing rouge and lipstick, sitting on café terraces sipping wine, and dancing in the louche nightclubs of Montmartre.

The same forces which had such a profound effect upon architecture—Cubism, speed, the quest for inspiration from exotic sources outside the Western canon—helped to shape women's dress in the 1920s. Jean Patou was one of the first to perceive that the new mobility in women's lives produced in particular by the motor car would affect fashion, and at the beginning of the 1920s he shortened skirts to facilitate getting in and out of automobiles. Though some, such as the President of the University of Florida, declared that "short skirts are born of the Devil" there was no stopping their heavenward progression. In 1919 the average distance of the hem above the ground was six or seven inches; by 1927 it had reached the knee. At the same time the boned corset was abandoned and dresses became softer in contour, less structured, reflecting a new casualness in lifestyle.

The half-American high bohemian Nancy Cunard photographed in 1930 in the Paris composing room of her Hours Press, which published, among others, Samuel Beckett and Ezra Pound, wore a cloche that resembled a turban, while in *Self-Portrait (Tamara in the Green Bugatti)* of 1925, the painter Tamara de Lempicka sported a helmetlike version. (Nancy Cunard, Thérèse Bonney/Bibliothèque Historique de la Ville de Paris; *Tamara,* Private Collection.)

And girls, both young and old, did indeed "put away" their curls. The new bobbed hair worn by icons such as author Anita Loos and screen star Clara Bow, the "It Girl," led to a rain of tresses upon beauty salon floors. More often than not the freshly shorn heads disappeared beneath a close-fitting "cloche" or bell. The archetypal models were by the supreme Parisian modistes,

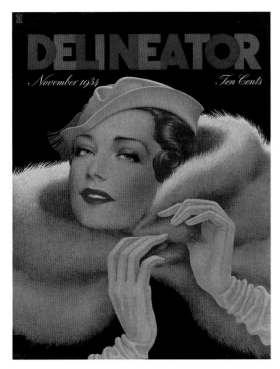

Reboux and Suzy, who modeled the felt to each customer's head. Well-off American women making their annual or semiannual shopping visit to Paris would routinely order the same hat in 12 different colors, in the same way that men purchased their standardized fedoras in black, gray, and brown. In both the pervasive presence of the cloche and the sleek coifs beneath them, there is a not-so-subtle Freudian concomitant. Like the replacement of the full-figured woman— exemplified by Lillian Russell in the previous generation—by the hipless, bustless silhouette, the boyish *garçonne* line of Lelong and Chanel, they evoked the all-male camaraderie of the trenches. Indeed an entirely new standard of female attractiveness emerged in the 1920s. Charlotte C. West, M.D., stated it unsparingly in her self-help volume, *Ageless Youth,* published in 1929: "To the American, slenderness is synonymous with beauty." The new woman was as active, as athletic, as any male. Whereas before the war women had played tennis in billowing dresses resembling tea gowns, couturiers like Dobbs on the Avenue Victor-Hugo now, for the first time, designed appropriate clothes for women to wear not only for tennis, but also for golf and skiing.

One of the notable characteristics of the Art Deco era was the dynamic interplay of the disciplines of painting, dance, architecture, and design with fashion. Diaghilev's Ballets Russes, which earlier had inspired Paul Poiret to abandon pastels for vivid colors, reappeared in Coco Chanel's "Slavic Period" with its elaborately embroidered peasant blouses. The painters Raoul Dufy and Sonia Delaunay designed dress fabrics and Delaunay also created men's dressing gowns and women's bathing costumes. The incomparable artist in lacquer, Jean Dunand, and Salvador

Indulgence in color is the chief privilege attending the Spring season. Both the Holeproof half-sock and Autogart are styled with this in mind...to allow full scope for individuality...to key the hosiery palette so that it will influence the whole accessory group...to encourage the fresh outlook within the limits of good taste. 35c to $1.00.

# HOLEPROOF HOSIERY

The man responsible for the brilliant Holeproof ad was the Russian-born Romain de Tirtoff, better known as Erte, shown here in 1926 in his Paris atelier. (Holeproof ad: Private

The Cubist influence on Art Deco is obvious in this 1928 ad for Van Heusen shirts and the 1932 ad for Holeproof Hosiery on the opposite page with its geometric-patterned polka-do

Men's fashions, too, were simplified in the 1920s, as shown by this 1924 illustration of the latest in male bathing costumes. (Private Collection.)

Dali painted fabrics for Elsa Schiaparelli, while the painter Jean Dupas created ads for *Vogue*, including a spectacular one for the Arnold Constable department store. In the spirit of the times, the milliner and couturiere Suzanne Talbot named her hats after artists, including one labeled "Claude Monet." This interaction between the arts cast an astonishingly wide net. The masterful metalworker Edgar Brandt inspired the fabric designs of Edouard Bénédictus, who with his *Les Jets d'Eau* translated Brandt's *Oasis* screen into brocade. The architect Robert Mallet-Stevens and artists such as Georges Braque, Max Ernst, Alberto Giacometti, and Alexander Calder designed jewelry. In a particularly felicitous leap between disciplines, the decorator and illustrator Pierre Legrain designed incomparable Art Deco bookbindings for the couturier Jacques Doucet using materials such as nickel, colored goatskin, and aluminum. One man in particular, Paul Iribe, exemplified this dynamic creative interplay. Trained as a commercial artist, Iribe worked briefly for Poiret, created sumptuous Art Deco furniture, was the interior decorator responsible for Jacques Doucet's fabled apartment, designed textiles, was a close friend and advisor to Chanel, and drew the logo—still used—for Jeanne Lanvin's Arpège. Iribe's career reached an astonishing climax when he journeyed to Hollywood and designed the avant-garde sets—filled with torches entwined by bronze cobras and mirrors framed by Deco batwings—for Cecil B. DeMille's 1921 hit, *The Affairs of Anatole*.

Many of New York's architects of the 1920s and 1930s were fully cognizant of the cutting-edge creativity of French fashion. William Van Alen freely used metal designs taken from textiles on the façade and around the entrances of his Chrysler Building and Ely Jacques Kahn, in stuctures such as 2 Park Avenue, designed in 1926, and the Indemnity Building on John Street of 1928, transcribed textiles into terra-cotta. Indeed, Francoise Bollack and Tom Killian, in their *Ely Jacques Kahn: New York Architect*, report that when Kahn was later queried about the sources of some of the motifs on his late 1920s buildings, he replied, "I was thinking of the texture of fabric."

The couturier most responsible for the astonishing appearance of the women on the avenue l'Opéra, as well as the women on Michigan Avenue and Fifth Avenue in 1925, was herself a woman whose life neatly epitomized the new era. Coco Chanel was born Gabrielle Chanel—she took her distinctive first name from the title of a popular song of her youth—in Saumur in the Loire Valley in 1883. Her father was a peddler, and after her mother's death, Chanel was sent to an orphanage run by Catholic nuns where she learned what proved to be the invaluable skills of sewing and embroidery.

She was a bright girl, and when she was 17 the sisters helped her obtain a scholarship to an excellent boarding school in the prosperous town of Moulins. "I was told that I must prepare myself for one of the three careers open to me: marriage, housekeeping, or dressmaking." At Moulins she quickly noticed not only the physiques and faces of the pupils attending the boys' school across the street, but their uniforms. They were all black with a simple belted jacket; the only touch of color was provided by their white shirts whose collars were worn outside the jacket. The ensemble was completed by loose black ties. "I discovered then," she recalled, "that black never goes out of fashion." The memory of those boys' school uniforms would surface time and again in Chanel's work.

Before long the very pretty young dressmaker was in business for herself, producing beautifully cut riding clothes for the officers of the aristocratic cavalry regiments stationed in the neighborhood. Soon she became the mistress of one of the officers, Étienne Balsan, and eventually went to live with him at his estate, Château de Royallieu, near Compiègne. Chanel eschewed the elaborate gowns of the day which she said resembled window curtains, and began designing her own clothes, clothes appropriate to the country life she was leading. Taking her designs to a local tailor in Compiègne, she was soon attracting notice with her simple, elegant suits, their short jackets not unlike those worn by jockeys. When other women asked who designed her clothes, Coco replied proudly that she did.

Coco Chanel is captured here in a 1930 watercolor by Cecil Beaton. (Private Collection.)

Chanel's dream had always been to have a shop in Paris, and with the backing first of Balsan, and later of her second lover, the wealthy English businessman, Arthur "Boy" Capel, she eventually opened one on the rue Cambon just behind the Ritz Hotel. Her first great success came with her hats, hats different from those anyone had seen before, hats with wide waving brims, low crowns, and, most startling of all, hats devoid of the traditional embellishments of the day—feathers, cabbage roses, tulle, and veils. "I had early learned the effect of subtraction in design."

In 1913 Capel underwrote Chanel's shop—the first with her name on the awning—in the fashionable racing and polo playing center of Deauville on the coast of Normandy. The resort was filled with sporting Englishmen, and at the track and on the polo field Chanel studied and absorbed their style: the perfectly tailored tweed jackets, the Fair Isle sweaters, the white flannels, the argyle-patterned hose. This *goût de'Anglais* she absorbed would have a profound effect on Chanel. "I noticed how natural and how comfortable their clothes were," she later told an interviewer. "I wished to design similar clothes for the life that women were beginning to live."

The outbreak of war in August 1914 facilitated Chanel's move to modernity. French government restrictions as to the amount of material that could be used to make a dress gave her an excuse to dramatically pare down her clothes and raise the hem above the ankle. The disappearance of luxury fabrics such as silk forced her to use a material originally manufactured for undergarments, wool jersey. "My idea now was style not adornment." The new simple silhouette combined with the surprising fabric was revolutionary. In order to save paper for the war effort, French fashion magazines had been shut down, so the first illustration of Chanel's creation appeared in 1916 in the American publication, *Harper's Bazaar*. The caption read, "Chanel's charming chemise dress." Coco Chanel's designs of brilliant simplicity, which, for the first time, created a style for all ages and for most classes, had a triumphal culmination in 1925 with the appearance of her little black dress. *Vogue* accurately predicted the transilient impact the design would have when it proclaimed that this dress was the "Ford" in every woman's closet.

With American women wearing the new stripped-down, jazzed-up "look" of Chanel, Patou, Doucet and others, many New York retailers were eager for shops whose design reflected the new mode. A dramatic illustration of the sea change in taste wrought by the Great War is the contrast between the commercial architecture on Fifth Avenue just north of 34th Street and that of the Avenue in the vicinity of 57th Street. In the precincts of 34th Street, which had originally been anchored by the old Waldorf-Astoria Hotel, the structures are redolent of the Belle Epoque. Here is the eight-story Beaux Arts emporium designed in 1906 by Trowbridge & Livingston for B. Altman's department store and here too is Stanford White's Italianate palazzo for the Gorham Company and his Venetian-inspired home for Tiffany, both also of 1906. As late as 1914 Starrett & Van Vleck had chosen an Italian Renaissance style, replete with pilasters, columns, balconies, and an overhanging copper cornice for the new Lord & Taylor store on Fifth Avenue at 38th Street.

The primary inspiration for retail outlets designed in a thoroughly new style came from the 1925 Paris Exposition. The design guidelines for the Exposition made it certain that its pavilions would be revolutionary: "Works admitted to the Exposition must show new inspiration and originality. . . . Reproductions, imitations, and counterfeits of ancient styles will be strictly prohibited." Since this was the first international fair at which manufacturing and machinery did not play a major part, fashion, interior design, and architecture took center stage. The pavilions of the four premier Paris department stores—Au Bon Marché by Louis Boileau, Grand Magasins du Printemps by Sauvage & Vybo, Grands Magasins du Louvre by Laprade, and Galeries Lafayette by Hiriart, Tribout, Beau—immediately attracted the attention of American businessmen and architects.

It did not take long for New York to match the Paris models with a number of outstanding small shops. Among the finest was Joseph Urban's store for the Bedell Company on West 34th Street of 1928. For this women's speciality salon, Urban drew ideas for his delicate ironwork from Parisian shop fronts such as that Azéma, Edrei, and Hardy had designed in 1926 for the hair salon of Girault on the boulevard des Capucines. But he also drew upon his Viennese background, and the

distinctive geometric decorative patterns of the upper floors owe a debt to Otto Wagner's structures on Vienna's Linke Wienzeile. Urban's elevator doors in the Bedell store—the dynamic
geometric forms of the doors themselves set beneath a painted illusionist classical pediment—
strikingly encapsulate Art Deco's grounding in the past and its commitment to the present.

Au Bon Marché pavilion at the 1925 Paris
Exposition. (Roger-Viollet.)

These new, eye-catching Deco shops brought a welcome frisson to New York streets. An
unabashedly Parisian style importation was presented by the premises of the perfumer
Delettrez at 580 Fifth Avenue. John Frederick Conan's 1927 façade was an elaborate composition
of black marble, metalwork that was a close copy of designs shown by Edgar Brandt at the 1925
Exposition, and that motif beloved by French Deco designers, baskets of stylized flowers, highly appropriate for a firm selling scent. In a similar vein, by 1929 the A. S. Beck Shoe Company,
which prided itself on making high-fashion, French-design shoes available at reasonable prices,
hired Vahan Hagopian and others to craft surprisingly innovative moderne shops in the French

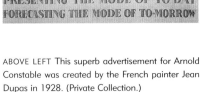

taste. But perhaps the most perfect melding of Art Deco architecture with a company business was the building which Charles A. Platt & Sons created in 1937 at the southwest corner of Fifth Avenue and 56th Street for the Steuben Division of Corning Glass. The elegant five-story limestone structure's decorative effect came solely from its two immense glass block windows, held in place by silver-colored frames, which brilliantly advertised both the beauty and the modernity of the firm's product.

A true virtuoso when it came to creating retail space and shop fronts in the Art Deco style was Ely Jacques Kahn. Born in New York in 1884, his distinctive name reflected his father's Austrian background and his mother's French heritage. Kahn attended Columbia University and then, in 1907, matriculated at the École des Beaux-Arts in Paris, where he entered the atelier of Gaston Redon, brother of the noted Symbolist painter, Odilon Redon. This somewhat unusual choice is not surprising, for early in life Kahn had ambitions of becoming an artist and, as his wife Liselotte wrote in her memoirs of 1996, he was in fact "a master watercolor painter." Throughout his career Kahn would daringly attempt to combine color with modern architecture. One of the high points of his stay in the French capital was a visit to the rue Fleurus salon of the American writer and art collector Gertrude Stein with its Cubist paintings by Braque, Derain, and Picasso. After returning to New York in 1911, Kahn taught design and held minor posts in a number of architects' offices until, through family connections, he met Albert Buchman. Buchman was head of Buchman & Fox, a firm noted for designing, among other things, department stores. Kahn joined the firm and after the retirement of Mortimer Fox in 1915, Buchman & Fox became Buchman & Kahn.

Ely Jacques Kahn was particularly fortunate in the number of significant Fifth Avenue commissions which came to him. In 1927 he was the key designer in the transformation of one of the thoroughfare's most prestigious blocks, that lying between 57th and 58th streets. In 1882 George B. Post had built for Cornelius Vanderbilt II, eldest grandson of the Commodore, a sumptuous chateau at the northwest corner of Fifth Avenue and 57th Street, but 10 years later Cornelius and his wife, Alice, had Post and Richard Morris Hunt extend their residence north to 58th Street, increasing its size to an astounding 137 rooms. In 1925, with real estate taxes climbing to $129,120 a year on the largest city house ever constructed in America, Alice, now a widow, decided to sell the property to developers.

Behind a unifying white marble façade, Kahn designed spaces for eight separate stores, though Bergdorf Goodman quickly became the primary client. While the structure's reticent mansard roof echoes the much more dramatic ones of the Plaza Hotel to the west and the Savoy-Plaza to the east, the building's simplified elevations with their single string course and minimal cornice relate it to the work of contemporary Art Deco–inspired Parisian architects such as Michel Roux-Spitz. Bergdorf's interiors were on the whole in the Louis XIV and French Empire styles, but the mirrored fur salon clearly revealed the impact on Kahn of the 1925 Paris Exposition. The architect reported that the fair's "succession of interiors of modern taste" had been "an awakening to me." Curiously, the very year, 1929, that Kahn was completing Bergdorf's traditional interiors, he was, at Fifth Avenue and 53rd Street, creating a sensational French moderne showroom for Van Cleef & Arpels, the jewelry firm which would eventually occupy the 57th Street side of the old Vanderbilt site. Van Cleef's square walnut boiseries in the manner of the *ébéniste* René Joubert, panels of Art Deco foliage, hanging silver and sand-blasted frosted glass lighting fixtures, and cubistic patterned upholstery paid unmistakable homage to the interiors by Maurice Dufrêne and others which had so impressed Kahn in Paris.

In 1930 Kahn organized his own firm, Ely Jacques Kahn Architects, and the next year collaborated with the renowned Finnish designer Eliel Saarinen on the Richard Hudnut salon. Occupying a narrow 25-foot-wide lot on Fifth Avenue between 54th and 55th Streets, Hudnut's vestigial fluted pilasters rising to a subtle Deco frieze, its bold geometric fenestration, and its interiors enriched with exotic materials, such as zebrawood, a strongly grained tropical wood favored by furniture designers like Paul Iribe, and gold leaf and nickel gave the small structure an impressive Parisian elegance.

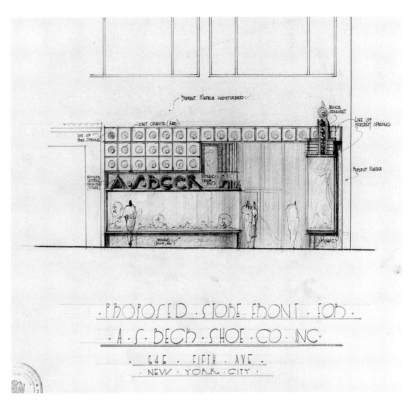

Deco readily lent itself to providing eye-catching shop fronts for small chain stores like those of the A. S. Beck Shoe Company. (Avery Architectural and Fine Arts Library, Columbia University.)

72. Vanderbilt Mansion, 58th Street and 5th Ave.
Series 1914 by Lynn C. Skeels

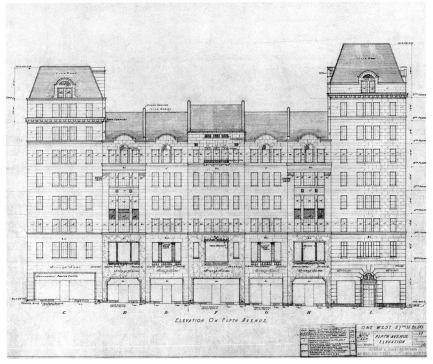

ELEVATION ON FIFTH AVENUE

ABOVE The demolition of the 137-room Cornelius Vanderbilt II mansion on Fifth Avenue between 57th and 58th streets in 1926 and its replacement in 1928 by Buchman & Kahn's Bergdorf Goodman store was a key event in the commercialization of midtown Fifth Avenue. (Canadian Centre for Architecture, Montreal.)

LEFT Rendering of the Fifth Avenue façade of Buchman & Kahn's Bergdorf Goodman Store. (Avery Architectural and Fine Arts Library, Columbia University.)

OPPOSITE Deco readily fit the requirements of medium-size commercial buildings, such as the one at the southwest corner of Fifth Avenue and 56th Street by Charles A. Platt & Sons for the Steuben Division of Corning Glass. The modish structure gave way in 1959 to a new, much larger Corning Glass Building. (Library of Congress.)

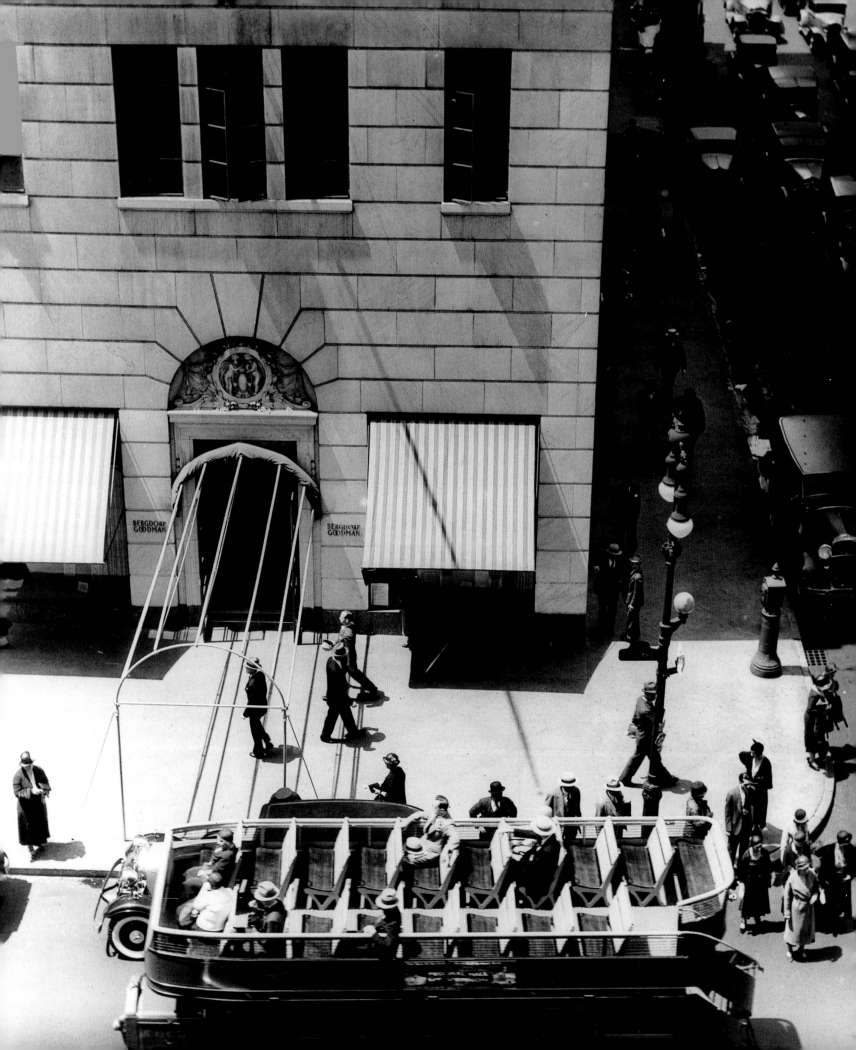

The indubitable crown jewel of Fifth Avenue's Art Deco retail establishments was the Stewart & Company store at the northwest corner of Fifth Avenue and 56th Street designed in 1929 by Warren & Wetmore. (Stewart & Company, founded in 1911, had been at 37th Street and Fifth Avenue.) Among New York's most prestigious architectural firms, Warren & Wetmore had been responsible for a number of the city's supreme Beaux Arts structures, among them the New York Yacht Club on West 44th Street of 1901 and Grand Central Terminal of 1913. Its senior partner, Whitney Warren, had not only attended the École des Beaux-Arts, but regularly visited Paris and was intrigued by the school's stylistic evolution toward a modernity based on classical precepts. The Stewart store, from its high square entrance to its windows set in grooves between expanses of unadorned walls that read as piers, to its crown of bold cubistic forms, was a brilliant interplay of geometric volume. A touch of decoration was provided by a pair of Deco bas-reliefs which terminated the thrust of the two central piers. The Crash wrote *finis* to Stewart & Company, and in 1930 Ely Jacques Kahn was brought in to remodel the structure for Bonwit Teller. Kahn deftly simplified the entrance to make it more welcoming by replacing Warren & Wetmore's somewhat fussy grilles with one consisting of a single rhythmically repeated Deco motif. Inside, in the entrance lobby, he cleared away a jumble of boutiques and replaced them with a terrazzo-floored lobby whose modern style was at one with the *à la page* fashions Bonwit's purveyed.

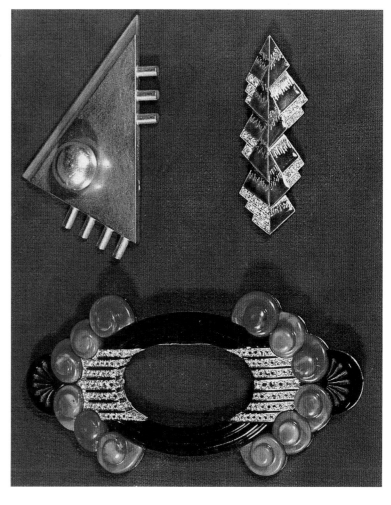

ABOVE Among the most stunning adaptations of Art Deco motifs in the fashion world was by jewelers, as shown by these three pieces, all of which date from 1925: a René-Charles Masse brooch for Boucheron using onyx, coral, and diamonds; a Georges Fouquet triangular gold brooch; and a platinum brooch of diamonds and green enamel by Raymond Tempier. (Private Collection.)

OPPOSITE A double-decker bus passes Bergdorf's Fifth Avenue and 58th Street corner in the 1930s. (Photograph by Irving Browning, New-York Historical Society.)

Not a few of the smart items of apparel which delighted customers in the shops of Fifth and other avenues had their origins in New York's vibrant world of fabric wholesalers, cloak-and-suit and women's dress manufacturers, and furriers. The owners of these businesses, intimately connected with the European fashion world, particularly that of Paris, desired buildings which would garner as much floor space as the zoning regulations permitted, but buildings whose decorative touches would also signal that the firms within were aesthetically up-to-date. In 1928 Ely Jacques Kahn designed at 261 Fifth Avenue, the southeast corner of 29th Street, a structure which spectacularly personified this melding of hard-headed economics and subtle taste. Seventy-five percent of the yellow brick 26-story edifice was a mix of showrooms and offices, with 25 percent given over to manufacturing. Two Sixty One reflects both the aesthetics of the 1925 Paris Exposition and Kahn's "dream of a colored city, buildings in harmonious tones making great masses of beautiful pattern." The structure's lower floors are embellished with woven textilelike patterns created by the vertical designs of the piers and the horizontal ones of the spandrels in gray and ochre terra-cotta with touches of bright gold. The lobby is an amazing Deco chamber of glistening gold on its upper walls and ceiling and spectacular red, gold, and green mosaics.

Not far from 261 Fifth Avenue, along West 29th and 30th streets, in the old Fur District, the rapid evolution in the 1920s of loft buildings toward an Art Deco style is vividly illustrated. There were ample funds to fuel this aesthetic revolution, for in these streets in the 1920s and 1930s the value of pelts handled—ranging from muskrat and rabbit to mink and ermine—annually averaged some 200 million dollars. The district employed 15,000 workers. At 216 West 29th Street, Henry I. Oser, a Russian-born architect responsible for numerous large midtown buildings, designed in 1925 a structure with a typical potpourri of stores, offices, showrooms, and workroom space. The massing, in its strong geometric plasticity, reflects the new zoning regulations and looks forward to the Deco, while the building's decoration is unabashedly Gothic Revival. But across the street, at 249, Oser not only gave his 15-story loft building Deco Cubist massing, but also, above the traditional coats of arms on the façade, moved into pure Deco decoration on the setbacks. Just how quickly the styles of Paris penetrated the district is shown by 207–209 West 29th Street of 1927, on the southwest corner of 7th Avenue. Here in a slender L-shaped brick loft building, with façades on 29th Street and on 7th Avenue, the architects, Sugarman & Berger, fashioned a striking sharp-edged 21-story structure with powerful geometric setbacks whose upper stories are topped by minimalist balustrades. The edifice's two intersecting slabs may be seen as ancestors of the knife-thin verticality of Rockefeller Center's RCA Building.

The dominance in the 1930s of Deco commercial design is exemplified by two stores for firms which encompassed the full spectrum of the retail market. Samuel Henry Kress, founder, president, and later chairman of S. H. Kress, a company with more than 200 five-and-ten-cent emporiums scattered across the United States, decided in the mid-1930s to construct a flagship store on Fifth Avenue at 39th Street. In *America's 5 & 10 Cent Stores: The Kress Legacy*, Bernice L. Thomas explains the motive behind the decision: "Privately, within the company, the store on Fifth Avenue was referred to as Mr. Kress's monument to himself. F. W. Woolworth had built a monument to himself and his dime store chain in the form of the world's tallest building—an office building on lower Broadway, with space for company headquarters. Samuel Kress simply built the world's largest, grandest five-and-ten-cent store." The Kress company had been since 1929 constructing Impressive Art Deco–style buildings in places as far-flung as Sacramento, California, and Greensboro, North Carolina. The man responsible for these designs was Edward F. Sibbert, a Brooklynite who had been educated at the Pratt Institute and at Cornell's School of Architecture. Now Sibbert was given the opportunity to create a building as fine as any on his hometown's premier shopping street. The seven-story structure, constructed of the most luxurious materials available, stood on a base of dark Quincy granite which supported a ground floor of

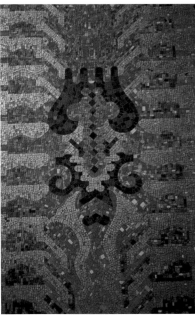

TOP At 261 Fifth Avenue, Ely Jacques Kahn is very much in the Art Deco tradition which emphasized the center of structures. Here this is achieved by the inviting receding planes above the entrance and by touches of metallic glazed terra-cotta, in this case gold luster. (Photograph by John Cadenhead.)

LEFT The lobby of 261 Fifth Avenue allowed Kahn to give free rein to both his love of color and his attraction to pre-Columbian ornamental motifs. The brilliantly hued glass mosaics provide the chamber with a shimmering and exciting wildness. (Photograph by John Cadenhead.)

RIGHT This intricately designed hanging glass and metal lighting fixture in the lobby of 261 Fifth Avenue reflects another important aspect of Kahn's artistic makeup, the profound influence on him of the 1925 Paris Exposition. The lamp relates closely to the elaborate lighting fixtures of French Art Deco designers such as Paul Kiss and Paul Follot. (Photograph by John Cadenhead.)

light-colored Mount Airy granite, and above that, an entire façade of fine white South Dover marble. The Kress store, with its bold grooves and paired bands of windows, exemplified Art Deco verticality. To emphasize this verticality, Sibbert used color to sharply differentiate the bands of windows from the building's light façade. The spandrels between the windows were of dark granite with the convex windows themselves tinted to match the spandrels. In addition, the grooves of windows broke through the roof line in the manner of some Deco skyscrapers. In order to assure that this extraordinary five-and-dime had, in the words of an advertisement, "Fifth Avenue Quality," the architect employed the highest-grade bronze to frame the windows and doors, while all the ornament on the Kress store was the work of René Chambellan. The very year the store opened, 1935, Chambellan completed the sculpture for the fountains in Rockefeller Center's Channel Gardens. Inside, one of Kress's glories was the moderne style basement cafeteria, decorated with 28 scenes of Old New York by Edward Trumbull, the artist responsible for the murals on the ceiling of the Chrysler Building's lobby.

By the close of the 1930s, New York's premier jewelers, Tiffany & Company, had decided to vacate Stanford White's version of Michele Sanmicheli's Palazzo Grimani at 37th Street and move uptown to the southeast corner of Fifth Avenue and 57th Street. Designed by Cross & Cross, the architects of the exuberantly decorated RCA Victor Building of 1931 on Lexington Avenue, the new Tiffany & Co. store was *sans* exuberant decoration, but it was nevertheless a subtle and attractive composition. The chief ornament on the seven-story granite and marble edifice was a clock supported by Atlas which had originally graced the façade of a Tiffany store on Union Square in the 1850s.

The Tiffany store, as was appropriate for a building which opened in 1940, marked the final phase of Art Deco's evolution to a stripped-down modern classicism. Its piers—distinctly separated by recessed rows of windows—rise to a delicately decorated cornice, assuming the role of columns, a ghostly echo of those on the façade of the emporium the firm had just quitted. The sense of classical symmetry is reinforced on the ground floor by the fact that all of the windows and entrances are kept to the same height. The doorways are given architectural emphasis by the use of broad moldings, while the show windows are reduced to a scale practical for the display of diamonds and pearls by the device of a window within a window, a technique that had been used by Robert Mallet-Stevens in 1928 at his Bally shoe store on the boulevard de la Madeleine in Paris.

In the late 1930s, the British photographer and designer, Cecil Beaton, was enthralled by the vibrant atmosphere encompassing New York's retail establishments: "Even Paris cannot compare with New York for the entertainment value of its shopping. . . . The window-dressing is one of the city's chief features. Each new fashion lives brilliantly, but dies an early death, in the shop-windows, as the seasons of the year pass prematurely. In this clean, new world Christ is born in November, and Bergdorf Goodman has robbed surrealism of its novelty before Dalí's new exhibition."

RIGHT An overlooked example of superb Art Deco architecture is the Lexington Avenue building of Bloomingdale's, seen here in 1935. The addition to the department store's mélange of Victorian and Romanesque Revival structures was the 1930 work of Starrett & Van Vleck. (Private Collection.)

OPPOSITE In 1940 Tiffany & Co. opened its new store by Cross & Cross at the Southeast corner of Fifth Avenue and 57th Street. (Private Collection.)

SHOPS AND SHOPPING À LA MODE

# ON THE TOWN: DRINKING, DINING, AND DANCING

The two images are truly worlds apart, as different in their way as a photograph of the coronation of Nicholas II, last Czar of all the Russias in Moscow, in 1896, and one taken in New York in 2004 of a gathering of Prime Ministers and Presidents at the United Nations. The first image is of the wildly extravagant ball—the cost was estimated to be more than $200,000—given by James Hazen Hyde at Sherry's on Fifth Avenue in the winter of 1895. The décor of the rooms hired for the evening and the dress of the ladies present were said to be inspired by the style of the court of Louis XVI at Versailles. In the photograph a group of ball goers poses for the professional picture taker with a faintly ironic stiffness. The men, including the famed Gilded Age architect, Stanford White, are impeccably attired in white tie and tails; the ladies, among them the enfant terrible of New York society, Mrs. Stuyvesant "Mamie" Fish, are extravagantly gowned in silk, satin, and lace confections of a vaguely "Louis" caste. In their hands are fans, held like wizard wands which might magically whisk them backward to the ancien régime, a world of titles and prerogatives, which New York's 400 strove mightily to both emulate and resuscitate.

The second image is of the mid-1930s. Henry and Clare Boothe Luce are seated at a table in El Morocco, 154 East 54th Street. We know that it is El Morocco because of the distinctive fake zebra skin upholstery on the banquette behind them. Jerome Zerbe, inventor of the candid-camera society photograph, has snapped the Luces, not looking out at the viewer the way the Hyde Ball attendees did, but in profile, gazing at one another. Henry Luce sports all the proper male regalia of the Deco age: black tie—far more casual than white—satin lapels, tasteful cuff links. In his right hand he holds not a wizard's wand but that ubiquitous symbol of thirties sophistication, a burning cigarette, while his left hand—its little finger adorned with a ring—is clutched in a fist, unconsciously revealing the power of a man who founded *Time* and *Fortune* and *Life* and who could forsake the strictures of his Presbyterian upbringing to divorce his first wife and indulge in the pleasure of punishing the parquet at El Morocco. Clare, his new wife, radiates Deco elegance: fashionably thin, her clinging slip dress cut deep enough to highlight her beautiful neck, her shimmering hair flat to her head, *à la mode* bangles on her wrists, and in her left hand, a cigarette, in this instance a symbol of a liberated woman, one who could insouciantly change husbands and creeds, and write a good play, titled, significantly, *The Women*.

The chasm separating this pair of beguiling *tableaux vivants* was created by two sociologically cataclysmic events: the First World War and Prohibition. The reluctant entry on April 6, 1917, of the United States into the Great War three years after Europe's death mills had begun finely grinding, would have consequences totally unforeseen for America. While the American, some 100,000, should not be minimized, they seem almost negligible when compared to the 1,400,000 French and 950,000 English dead. But for the more than 2,000,000 doughboys for whom the most exciting event in their lives, until then, had been a church social in Missouri or a ride on the Ferris wheel at Chicago's White City amusement park or a day at New York City's

Coney Island, disembarking from their ships at Brest or St. Nazaire and stepping into a world at war would be a transforming experience.

One of them was an 18-year-old journalist from Oak Park, Illinois, who in December of 1917 had volunteered to be a Red Cross ambulance driver. Ernest Hemingway was eager to get into the fight and when he arrived in Paris in early June, 1918, and found the city being bombarded by the Germans' long-range Paris guns, he ordered a dumbfounded taxi driver to take him to "where those shells are falling." So excited was he by the dramatic panoply of war that Hemingway could coolly write his parents: "The mother of a man that has died for his country should be the proudest woman in the world, and the happiest." After two days in Paris, he was assigned to the Italian front northwest of Venice. There on July 8, Hemingway was seriously wounded in both legs by shrapnel from an Austrian mortar shell which landed three feet away. The experience would resurface in *A Farewell to Arms*: "I heard a cough, then came the chuh-chuh-chuh-chuh—then there was a flash, as when a blast-furnace door is swung open, and a roar that started white and went red and on and on in a rushing wind." In time this physical experience of battle would expunge its perceived glamour. "The truth about war," Hemingway wrote later, "was lacking to me when I needed it most."

Undoubtedly the most famous American expression of the pervasive fatalism which enveloped those who served for extended periods at a front where thousands died trying to gain a few yards of ground was written by a young New Yorker and Harvard graduate, Alan Seeger. Like Hemingway, Seeger was anxious to join in the fight. But for the New Yorker, the impetus came not alone from the sense of excitement that the war engendered, but also from a conviction that he should be battling on the side, as he perceived it, of civilization. Thus in 1914, Seeger took a route that was taken by many other Americans in the years before the United States entered the war and joined the French Foreign Legion. His poem, "I Have a Rendezvous with Death" is a haunting ballad of pending mortality:

> I have a rendezvous with Death
> At some disputed barricade,
> When Spring comes back with rustling shade
> And apple-blossoms fill the air—
> I have a rendezvous with Death
> When Spring brings back blue days and fair. . . .

The verses were published in the *New Republic* in 1916. Seeger, along with 600,000 other Allied soldiers, kept his rendezvous that same year during the Battle of the Somme. The date was July 4.

The sense of civilization pulled up by its roots, of the irrelevance of all past standards, and of every former formula for deportment, plays through the poems, short stories, and novels of the American writers of the so-called "Lost Generation," writers like Hemingway, John dos Passos, and e. e. cummings, who served in the war. It is also a recurring theme of those who were not there, like F. Scott Fitzgerald. Significantly, in his quintessential novel of the 1920s, *Tender Is the Night*, Fitzgerald has one of his central characters, Dick Diver, conduct two others on a tour of a battlefield in Northern France: "See that little stream—we could walk to it in two minutes. It took the British a month to walk to it—a whole empire walking very slowly, dying in front and pushing forward behind. And another empire walking very slowly backward a few inches a day, leaving the dead like a million bloody rugs."

The First World War smashed to bits the universe of the James Hazen Hyde Ball just as unequivocally as it smashed to bits Hohenzollern Berlin and Belle Epoque Paris and Edwardian London, giving the critical shove down that slippery slope which ended with British dukes and earls being little more than innkeepers for the day-trippers traipsing through their palaces.

When at the 11th hour of the 11th day of the 11th month of 1918, the Armistice was signed, bringing to a close "The War to End Wars," "The War to Make the World Safe for Democracy," the doughboys returned to a nation where it was not legal to have an alcoholic drink. After Pernods at La Coupole and Le Dôme in Montparnasse and bottles of Sancerre at the Moulin Rouge in Montmartre, this seemed a rather dry welcome. Ironically, Prohibition had gotten its big push during the conflict when those in favor of draining America's watering holes argued that banning demon rum would conserve grain needed to feed the world and that workers would have steadier hands to make guns and bombs if they could not get those hands on a glass of whiskey or gin or on a stein of beer. It was made permanent, or so it was thought at the time, and nationwide, by the 18th Amendment to the Constitution which was declared ratified on January 29, 1919. Prohibition represented a triumph of the values of America's small town and rural-based Protestant denominations, particularly the Methodist and Baptist churches in the South and Midwest, and of the Women's Christian Temperance Union founded in Illinois and the Anti-Saloon League founded in Ohio. At the same time, it was a not-so-subtle slap in the face of Irish Catholics with their saloons; the Germans, who were prominent in the brewing and distilling industries; as well as Jews and those Protestant denominations, particularly Unitarians and Episcopalians, who were anti-Prohibition. In metropolises like New York and Chicago, where those opposed to the new amendment constituted the vast majority of the populace and where it was estimated that more than half the people made a daily visit to a saloon, the new law was greeted with astonishment and outrage. It should be noted that New York's two favorite politicians, Mayor Jimmy "Beau James" Walker and Governor Alfred E. "Al" Smith were confirmed "wets." Most New Yorkers unreservedly agreed with Walker's picturesque characterization of do-gooders of all stripes: "A reformer is a guy who rides through a sewer in a glass-bottomed boat."

The allure of Paris in the 1920s, stemming from the pro-French feelings nourished by the First World War, the freedom Paris gave American artists, and the fact that Prohibition was unknown in the "City of Light," was personified by the great black American dancer and singer, Josephine Baker. Her appearance in *La Revue Negre* at the Theâtre des Champs-Élysées in 1925 took Paris by storm. In this 1927 hand-colored lithograph, the French artist Paul Colin captures Baker's electric, sensual energy. (Private Collection.)

The night that Prohibition went into effect, January 16, 1920, was icily cold in Gotham, the thermometer hovering just above zero. The question asked time and again by saloon keepers, bartenders, and lovers of the grape and grain, of Congressmen like Christopher D. Sullivan of the East Side, was "Are they really going to enforce it?" From dives on the Bowery to the elegant Adam-style dining room of the Ritz-Carlton on Madison Avenue and the stag-horn–decorated Hunt Room of the Astor on Times Square the atmosphere was funereal. Indeed some watering holes went so far as to mail out black-edged invitations to attend the "Last rites for our dear departed spirit, John Barleycorn," where waiters dressed as pallbearers placed drinks atop a real coffin. Panhandlers on Broadway got an enthusiastically positive response when they asked for "a quarter for a last drink."

In the midst of the gloom brought on by the contemplation of the impending drought, New York's preeminent brothel keeper, Polly Adler, declared that when it came to Gotham, "They might as well try to dry up the Atlantic with a post office blotter." The lady was correct. As Edward Robb Ellis reported in his invaluable 1966 study, *The Epic of New York City*: "Before Prohibition a man could get a drink in 15,000 places in town, but soon thereafter 32,000 illegal New York establishments sold liquor. There weren't enough federal Prohibition agents, many were inefficient, and some were downright corrupt." Al Capone, a Brooklyn boy, promptly took the train for Chicago to help assuage the thirst of the Windy City, but New York suffered no dearth of bootleggers. Long Island, with its coastline conveniently endowed with countless havens and harbors from Montauk to Glen Cove, as well as the Jersey shore with dockage from Long Branch to Cape May, provided ideal landing places for illegal booze. By 1925 the syndicate run by Waxey Gordon had superb navigational charts and ship-to-shore radios to guide its ships transporting top quality Scotch from Nova Scotia. One transaction netted a whopping $240,000. Ships also came in from the island of Bimini, in the straits of Florida, and Belize, the capitol of British Honduras, loaded with gin and rum which were quickly off-loaded to replenish the supplies and fortunes of characters curiously similar to Fitzgerald's Jay Gatsby. The United States Department of Commerce estimated that by the mid-1920s the value of the liquor being smuggled into the country averaged 40 million dollars a year.

The absurdities and hypocrisies of the United States in the 1920s and early 1930s, as exemplified by Prohibition, were a ready target for the wit of New Yorkers and other urbanites. Franklin Pierce Adams (F.P.A.), whose brilliant column "The Conning Tower" appeared in the *New York World*, deliciously satirized America's conflicted attitude toward the "noble experiment":

> *Prohibition is an awful flop.*
> *We like it.*
> *It can't stop what it's meant to stop.*
> *We like it.*
> *It's left a trail of graft and slime,*
> *It's filled our land with vice and crime*
> *It don't prohibit worth a dime,*
> *Nevertheless we're for it.*

While Prohibition was a flop from the point of view of law enforcement, it was an unmitigated success when it came to inspiring new concepts for drinking and socializing. Both the speakeasy and the nightclub owe their birth to it. The first devolved from the "speak-softly shop," a 19th-century English phrase denoting a seaside smuggler's cottage. By the late 1880s "speakeasy" was being used across America to describe an establishment where one could buy liquor in dry counties, like, ironically, Bourbon County, Kentucky, and dry states like Mississippi. But "speakeasy" entered the national vocabulary in the 1920s when it was employed to designate a dark, poorly ventilated dive, usually in a basement, entry to which was permitted only after the would-be imbiber spoke easily, that is softly, a password, while being observed through a peephole.

By 1933, the police estimated that there were 9,000 speakeasies in New York City, ranging from modest joints like the one on Broadway near City Hall, popular with Tammany Democrats, to those ensconced in the wood-paneled parlors of the old brownstones which lined the streets of the West 50s. Here the price of a drink was a not inconsiderable one dollar, and tipplers rubbed shoulders with Vanderbilts and Whitneys. West 52nd Street, with a grand aggregate of 38 speakeasies, proudly billed itself as the "wettest block in Manhattan." Among its more elegant establishments was that run by Jack Kriendler at 21 West 52nd Street, which opened for business on January 1, 1930. Kriendler's saloon survived to witness the end of Prohibition and transmogrified into the glamorous "21" restaurant patronized by the likes of Humphrey Bogart and Jack and Jackie Kennedy.

A vivid vignette of speakeasy life is painted by John Keats in *You Might As Well Live*, the biography of the short story writer, poet, and Algonquin Round Table wit, Dorothy Parker. The speakeasy visited is most likely Jack and Charlie's Puncheon Club, 42 West 49th Street, a high-class boîte which served top brand name spirits that had not been "guillotined," that is, cut with cheap alcohol. Parker's pals are two other members of the Algonquin Round Table, the zany humorist and drama critic Robert Benchley and the screenwriter Donald Ogden Stewart, whose credits include *The Philadelphia Story*. Keats wrote:

> In the late afternoon of such a day, Mrs. Parker might accompany Mr. Benchley and Mr. Stewart to a brownstone on the West Side. They would somewhat furtively descend the basement steps, and Mr. Stewart would ring for admission. A sliding panel in the steel door would snick back, revealing a peephole. Mr. Stewart, if not recognized to be a regular patron of the establishment, would have to mutter, "Joe sent me," or otherwise give a password, and if all went well, there would be a noise of bolts and chains, the door would slip quickly open and be as quickly shut, chained and bolted behind them. They would find themselves in a dark room, thick with cigarette smoke and loud with drunken voices, themselves now part of an illicit camaraderie which might very well include the cop on the beat. . . .

The presence of Mrs. Parker in the Puncheon Club dramatically illustrates a totally unexpected consequence of the 18th Amendment, a consequence which deftly shot another arrow into the

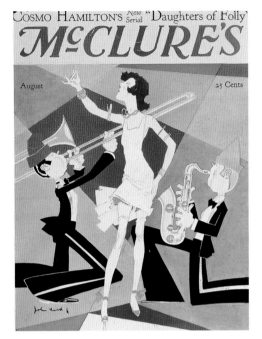

expiring body of Old New York Society. Stanley Walker, the ubiquitous city editor of the *New York Herald Tribune*, lays out the scenario in *The Night Club Era*, published in 1933: "Soon after 1920 great, ravening hordes of women began to discover what their less respectable sisters had known for years—that it was a lot of fun, if you liked it, to get soused. All over New York these up and coming females, piled out of their hideaways, rang the bells of speakeasies, wheedled drugstores into selling them gin and rye, and even in establishments of great decorum begged their escorts for a nip from a hip flask." Before Prohibition even a female as quick-witted and self-possessed as Dorothy Parker would not have been served in a New York bar.

The advent of women on the toxicant circuit affected not only the way Americans drank, but the relationship between the sexes as well. This sea change is encapsulated in F. Scott Fitzgerald's memorable short story, "Babylon Revisited," where Charlie Wales attempts to regain custody of his young daughter from his in-laws in Paris after he and his wife have ruined their lives drinking: "You know I never did drink heavily until I gave up business and came over here with nothing to do. Then Helen and I began to run around. . . ." It suddenly became de rigueur for those living on Park and Fifth Avenues to serve cocktails before dinner; the concoctions offered ran the gamut from the traditional martini and Manhattan to the newly fashionable sidecar, brandy Alexander, and pink lady.

Once Prohibition desiccated the bars, dining rooms, and ballrooms of New York's hotels, those introducing their daughters to Society at the Ritz or Plaza hired private suites in the caravansaries where debutantes and their male escorts could quaff champagne to their heart's

ABOVE LEFT No artist caught the kinetic energy of the Jazz Age better than John Held, Jr. (Culver Pictures, Inc.)

ABOVE RIGHT Will Cotton's 1929 pastel captures the famed Thanatopsis Pleasure and Inside Straight Club, which met weekends at the Algonquin Hotel. Among the plethora of well-known writers and actors Dorothy Parker and Robert Benchley are on the left, George S. Kaufman and Eddie Cantor are on the right, while presiding over the card table in the center is Alexander Woollcott. Harpo Marx, to the right of Woollcott, was a regular, but brother Groucho, who never attended, quipped, "The admission fee is a viper's tongue and a half-concealed stiletto." (Courtesy of Anne Kaufman Schnieder.)

ABOVE LEFT Art Deco's enthrallment with modern transportation surfaced in unexpected ways. This 1920s German-made cocktail shaker in the shape of a zeppelin, when taken apart, reveals a set of spoons, a flask, a corkscrew, and a shot measure. The 1920s smoking set in the form of an airplane could also be disassembled, producing a cigar-cutter, three ashtrays, and two cigarette cases. (Private Collection.)

RIGHT Prohibition, ironically, helped to glamorize drinking. This handsome 1938 Deco advertisement for champagne brilliantly combines the elegance of the glass which will hold the delicious bubbly with the smart white-tie-garbed gentleman who will happily quaff it. (Private Collection.)

OPPOSITE TOP  Deco female sophistication is embodied to the nth degree in this illustration from the August 1925 issue of the French publication *Revue Mensuelle*. All the essential elements are present: décolleté gown, bobbed hair, cascading earrings, and a burning cigarette. (Private Collection.)

OPPOSITE BOTTOM Program of the Cotton Club 1931. The famed club opened in 1923 at 142nd Street and Lenox Avenue in Harlem. The waiters and the extraordinary talent--which included Duke Ellington, Cab Calloway, Lena Horne, and Ethel Waters--were black, but the owners and audience were white. One of the reasons for the Cotton Club's success was the fact that its last show started after those of downtown clubs finished, so it became the place to go for entertainers like Eddie Cantor, Milton Berle, and Jimmy Durante. The Cotton Club closed its doors in 1936. (Private Collection.)

content. The well-lubricated high jinks which ensued were vociferously condemned by a number of Gotham's most fearsome dowagers, including Mrs. J. Pierpont Morgan and Mrs. Henry Phipps. Coincidentally with the freedom of women to drink came the freedom to smoke. There had, in fact, been vociferous opposition to permitting females to puff in public. The nay-sayers had been quelled when a Bronx judge exonerated a woman charged with smoking in the street with the quip: "What do you think this is, Hicksville?" The image of the new woman, this flapper, chic, svelte, swell, clasping an exquisite holder of jade, onyx, or gold in which smoldered a slender cigarette, smoke rising from it like incense for the gods, is one of the defining advertising metaphors of the Deco decades.

Speakeasies, as a rule, served food, though it might be nothing more than chop suey sent up from Mott Street, but they did not have entertainment. For that, those out for a night on the town had to head to one of the new clubs. Stanley Walker credits the seminal idea of combining the old-fashioned cabaret restaurant with a featured dance team which could flawlessly execute the new steps, such as the fox-trot and Charleston, and packaging it in an establishment with a restricted membership, a nightclub, to the now-forgotten Jules Ansaldi. The original idea was to re-create the ambience formerly provided by Gilded Age Gotham hangouts like Delmonico's and Sherry's, but the fact that the new clubs were selling illegal wines and spirits and thus had to be clandestine quickly made them far different from anything Charles Delmonico or Louis Sherry could have imagined. Some of the names—the Hyena, the Jail, the Ha-Ha—boldly reflected the dismissive attitude toward the law and traditional values embraced by many of New York's upper and not-so-upper crust after 1920.

A number of the clubs had stellar entertainment. Paul Whiteman and his orchestra played at the Palais Royal and Morton Downey at the Casanova; Clifton Webb and Mary Hay titillated packed houses with their brilliant comic dances at Ciro's, while at the Trocadero the brother and sister team of Fred and Adele Astaire wowed Gothamites with their terpsichorean perfection; Helen Morgan sang smoky love songs perched atop a piano in her own club on 54th Street, and Rudy Vallee elicited

New York's premier lady speakeasy proprietor, "Texas" Guinan, being escorted into a paddy wagon after a raid on one of her establishments. (Private Collection.)

sighs from the ladies when he crooned through a megaphone at the Heigh-Ho. If you sought laughter there was always Jimmy Durante at the Club Durant and Beatrice Lillie at the swank Sutton Club. If the reveler headed uptown to Harlem there was the bluesy orchestra of Duke Ellington with "Mood Indigo" at the Cotton Club on Lenox Avenue and Fats Waller playing his own "Ain't Misbehavin'" at Connie's Inn on Seventh. And if you longed for something that was truly *le dernier cri* there was the new vogue for the female impersonator, fueled by the astounding stardom of Barbette at the Casino de Paris, one of the top Parisian gathering places. Born Vander Clyde in Round Rock, Texas, Barbette was a superb athlete who performed sensational aerial feats on a high trapeze without a net while elegantly attired as a woman. In New York the place for that was the Club Pansy!

Jules Ansaldi had one serious competitor for the title "inventor of the nightclub": Mary Louise Cecilia Guinan from Waco, Texas. "Texas" Guinan played a whiz-bang game of poker, was universally liked, never missed mass, and, with her various clubs, one called, naturally, The Club Guinan, netted a rumored one million dollars a year. One of her show girls was Ruby Keeler, who got a real-life break in the film *42nd Street*. If a customer were lucky enough to have Guinan greet him with her world famous, "Hello, sucker!" his evening was made.

By the time—December 5, 1933—that the 21st Amendment to the Constitution, repealing the 18th Amendment and thus ending Prohibition, was declared ratified, Manhattan and the other boroughs were thirsting for it. The *New York Times* reported that the crews on ships in port, such as the German sailors on the *Bremen* and *Berlin*, cheered lustily because they could have wine and beer with their Christmas dinner. Longchamps excitedly proclaimed "Cocktails 25 cents and up!" The Waldorf-Astoria's Empire Room advertised "Cocktail and aperitif service"; the Palais Royal, Broadway and 48th Street, offered an Argentine Rhumba Orchestra, the Boswell Sisters, and the "choicest variety of wines and liquors"; the Hotel Pierre advised patrons that its new Neptune Room was the perfect rendezvous " for "The Cocktail Hour"; the St. George in Brooklyn Heights had dancing for New Year's Eve and a "choice selection of wines and liquor at very modest prices"; and Gallagher's Steak House on West 52nd Street notified customers that it was, for the first time in more than a decade, serving alcoholic drinks with its prime beef. The city's newspapers had given the panting public the good news that the State Alcoholic Beverage Control Board had announced that liquor stores could remain open Christmas and New Year's Days, but on December 24 reported the bad news that, with 2,460 licenses to sell alcoholic beverages having been issued in the three days since Repeal, "the limited stocks of legal liquor in the city were sold out completely."

Just as America would never be the same again, so the porcelain Humpty Dumpty of Old New York Society had been shattered and all the Social Register Queens and Kings could not put it back together again. Prohibition and the Great War had, of course, been salient factors in giving H.D. the push, but they had been mightily aided by taxes—income, inheritance, and real estate. The fact was that a significant section of society had deserted its somnolent clubs and ersatz châteaux and had begun to pow-wow in restaurants. Maury Paul, the impeccably credentialed, white-tie society reporter who was the Hearst newspapers' first Cholly Knickerbocker, fiercely laid claim to having freshly minted the defining label of the new dispensation, "café society." The story, as recounted in *Who Killed*

The first cargo of beer departs New York City's Jacob Rupert Brewery, Third Avenue at 92nd Street, after the end of Prohibition. (American Architectural Archives.)

*Society* by the preeminent chronicler of the *beau monde* Cleveland Amory, is that one evening in the old Ritz on Madison Avenue, Paul spied, dining together, the Philadelphian Joseph Widener, of traction and thoroughbreds; Laura Corrigan, a Chicago waitress, who after marriage to a Cleveland steel tycoon went to England and became a good friend of the royal family; Whitney Warren, Jr., the architect of Grand Central Terminal, in whose veins circulated a drop or two of Vanderbilt blood; and a passel of Goelets, who were both New York real estate barons and card-carrying members of the 400, dining together. Paul knew that he had been granted a revelation comparable in importance to that of Moses on Mount Sinai. "Society is not staying home and entertaining anymore. Society is going out to dinner, out to night life and letting down the barriers," he observed to a friend. "Heavens, that I should see a Widener, a Goelet, a Corrigan, and

One of the chief attractions of café society was the chance to rub elbows with the likes of Cole Porter and Elsa Maxwell, caught imbibing at the Stork, or with freshly minted celebrities like boxer Gene Tunney and Charles Lindbergh photographed in 1928 in the Manhattan apartment of society painter Charles Baskerville, who is standing between them. The previous year Tunney had retained his heavyweight title by defeating Jack Dempsey before a crowd of 100,000 in Chicago and "Lucky Lindy" had made his historic solo flight from Long Island to Paris. (All images, Private Collection.)

OPPOSITE Café society was born when New York's 400 began entertaining, not at home, but in restaurants and nightclubs. (American Architectural Archives.)

ABOVE  Glamour gal Brenda Frazier, New York's 1938 deb of the year. Miss Frazier's coming out party made the cover of *Life* magazine. (Private Collection.)

OPPOSITE  Art Deco as a style ran the whole gamut from costly pieces by Ruhlmann to the "Depression Modern" glass sold at five and dimes. Smart New York promoters of Tin Pan Alley songs and Broadway musicals quickly dropped images of roses and picket fences for a lively Art Deco style which encompassed flappers, sheiks, moderne designs, and the latest avant-garde lettering.

LEFT  Cover of the sheet music for Hoagy Carmichael and Mitchell Parish's 1928 dance hit, "Stardust." (Private Collection.)

RIGHT  Poster for the Henderson, DeSylva, and Brown boffo 1927 musical *Good News!* Among the show's dance-happy songs was "The Varsity Drag," a Charlestown-style number which instantly became a national craze. (Private Collection.)

a Warren all together." The next day, while writing his column, Maury Paul typed the two catalytic words, "café society." If the drawbridge across the *haut monde* moat was not all the way down, it was definitely down far enough so that the socially agile could readily leap the gap.

Paul was right about society not staying home. The hard fact was that most had no homes in which to stay. The relentless demolition in the 1920s and 1930s of the grand Fifth Avenue mansions marked the end of serious at-home entertaining in New York. The Fifth and Park Avenue apartments that Gotham's *gratin* moved into, be they ever so pretentious, were, at best, tenements for the rich. In the day when Caroline Webster Schermerhorn Astor could effortlessly offer after-opera dining and dancing for the entire 400 under her own ridgepole, the scribes of the society pages of the *Herald*, the *Tribune*, and the *Times* were suitably grateful for any crumb "the" Mrs. Astor could drop them: a guest list, a menu, or the color of the orchids festooning her board. But when the base for social operations shifted to restaurants and nightclubs, social life was transfigured. It must be pointed out, though, that not everyone dashed into the public spotlight. Helen Winslow—Mrs. John G. Winslow—of New York and Newport, a member of the distinguished Fahnestock family of bankers and brokers, who at one time occupied most of the sumptuous Villard Houses behind St. Patrick's Cathedral, sounds a note of mild disapproval: "Conservative New Yorkers didn't participate frequently in Café Society life, though, of course, they knew many of the individuals who did."

The reality was that once the younger generation had leapt the hurdles of Newport and New York and landed in the heady vortex of speakeasies and clubs where one literally rubbed shoulders with high-society bohemians like Gertrude Vanderbilt Whitney and Roger Kahn, cut-up son of banker Otto Kahn; silver screen lotharios like Valentino; scribes like Heywood Broun; long-legged Ziegfeld Follies showgirls; and young Mafia torpedoes just down from Sing-Sing, dinner at the yawningly proper Union Club, Knickerbocker, or Brook seemed pretty tame. Now, after Repeal, a new ingredient was added to the mix, a factor Cleveland Amory labeled "public-ciety." During Prohibition clubbing around town might be fun, but it was also illegal, so there was no recording of the night's events unless it was on a police blotter. After 1933, fear faded and those yearning to be considered a part of the "smart set" were thrilled to find their names and faces in at least one of Gotham's seven dailies. Maury Paul was right on the money with his advice after his secretary announced that she was quitting and going to Hollywood to find a job. Her only hesitation, she said, came from not wanting to have to sleep with a producer to get ahead. "My dear child," Paul shot back, "nobody gives a damn who you sleep with. In this world it's who you're seen dining with that counts."

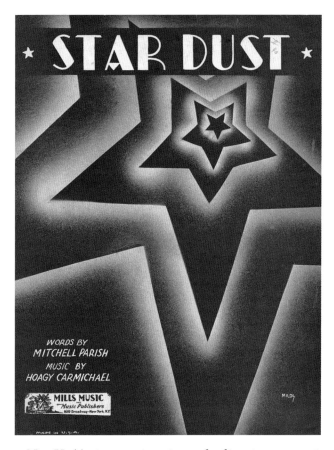

New York's tip-top triumvirate of café society venues in the 1930s were the Colony Restaurant on 61st Street near Madison Avenue, the Stork Club at 3 East 53rd Street, and El Morocco at 154 East 54th Street. The Colony, presided over by founders Gene Cavallero and Ernest Cerutti, was the prime hunting ground of Maury Paul in search of tidbits for the *New York American*. More restaurant than nightclub, the Colony was especially noted for serving, in season, the best Scotch grouse in town and the rarest of burgundies to accompany the gamy bird, and had a seating pecking order, in the words of one reporter, "the most arbitrary this side of the pew list of St. Thomas's Church." The right-hand corner table was inevitably reserved for William K. Vanderbilt, divorced from the formidable Alva, while other nearby tables were guarded, with the tenacity usually reserved for guarding season boxes at the Metropolitan Opera, by real estate heir William Rhinelander Stewart and Ellin Mackay Berlin, whose past included a fortune made by her grandfather in the Comstock silver lode and whose present included marriage to the composer of "Cheek to Cheek." The farther away from the door one was placed, the lower one's

ABOVE LEFT Theatergoers, sporting evening dresses, furs, and top hats, gather outside a Broadway
theater in the 1930s. (American Archives.)

ABOVE RIGHT Lucius Beebe, scribe extraordinaire,
whose beat was Gotham's nocturnal frolics.
(Courtesy Virginia Irvin.)

status, until, at the very back, behind a crimson damask curtain, was what the staff referred to *sotto voce* as "The Monkey House."

The Stork Club, with seating for 1,000, was a bit less exclusive than the Colony, but still selective enough that debs who were turned away were regularly spied rushing toward Fifth Avenue in floods of tears. The Stork was the favored corral of journalists like drama critic Richard Watts and writers like Damon Runyon, whose stories would be the basis of the glorious musical, *Guys and Dolls*. It also catered to the thoroughbred racing set in from Belmont or down from Saratoga, and was a prime destination for honeymooning out-of-towners who dreamt of receiving one of the prodigious purple orchid corsages which the Stork's owner, Sherman Billingsley, regularly handed out. Though Billingsley might be the owner, the *genius loci* of the Stork was Walter Winchell, whose column in the *Daily Mirror* was morning-after reading for café society celebrants. "Ah, I see you made Winchell this morning!" was a much-sought-after accolade, particularly if it referred to the prestigious Monday column. Winchell knew his power: "Social position is now more a matter of press than prestige," he quipped.

But café society's ultimate mecca, its inner sanctum, its holy of holies, was El Morocco, suavely supervised by John Perona, who had gathered a devoted following from the various saloons he had

*"Come along. We're going to the Trans-Lux to hiss Roosevelt."*

During the 1936 Roosevelt-Landon campaign the Trans-Lux audiences cheered and hissed, applauded and booed as the opposing candidates appeared on the screen. This 1936 *New Yorker* cartoon leaves no doubt as to the attitude of these Upper Eastsiders toward "that man in the White House." (© *The New Yorker Collection* 1936 Peter Arno from cartoonbank.com)

Architecturally, the most progressive New York movie theater chain was the Trans-Lux, which offered continuous 60-minute programs consisting of newsreels, brief comedies, and travelogues. The Trans-Lux, at the southwest corner of Lexington Avenue and East 52nd Street of 1938, by Thomas Lamb and Walker & Gillette, was a Deco extravaganza whose curved corner was enriched with a Mayan-inspired stepped design and radiating suns. (Library of Congress.)

Jerome Zerbe snaps a picture of Mrs. Sherman Jenney, standing, and Mrs. William Wetmore in El Morocco in 1938. (Photograph by Horst for *Vogue*, ©1938 Condé Nast Publications, Inc.)

operated in Manhattan during the dry years. With just half the seating capacity of the Stork, El Morocco was no paradise of easy entry. "In the thirties, El Morocco was considered the most exclusive nightclub in the city," the urbane *New Yorker* writer Brendan Gill recalled. "El Morocco was THE place to be seen, especially after the theatre. A queue of well-born, well-heeled people all armed with reservations would be willing to stand for long periods in the street until they could gain admission to the sacred place."

Gill's mention of the theater brings up what Brooks Atkinson, the noted drama critic of the *Herald Tribune* and, later, the *New York Times*, termed "The Paradox of the Thirties." For while the Depression chopped the number of productions from 239 for the 1929–1930 season to 187 for 1930–1931, the decade was a period of astonishing Broadway creativity. It was the time of Eugene O'Neill's *Ah, Wilderness!* with George M. Cohan and Gene Lockhart, of Maxwell Anderson's *Mary of Scotland* with Helen Hayes and Helen Menken, of Sidney Howard's dramatization of Sinclair Lewis's *Dodsworth*, starring Walter Huston, of Robert Sherwood's *The Petrified Forest*, starring Leslie Howard, of Noël Coward's *Private Lives*, featuring the playwright and Gertrude Lawrence, of Lillian Hellman's The *Children's Hour*, and of Clifford Odets's *Awake and Sing!* It was also the era of sublime musicals: Cole Porter's *Anything Goes*, George Gershwin and George S. Kaufman's Let 'Em Eat Cake, and Jerome Kern's *Roberta*, to name but three. Essayist and critic John Mason Brown summed up the paradox with the phrase "these full lean years." It should also be noted that the Depression failed to fray the New York theaters' rigid dress code. Helen Josephy and Mary Margaret McBride, in their 1931 guidebook, *New York Is Everybody's Town*, warn visitors: "New Yorkers wear evening clothes to revues or musical comedies that are hits, also to society comedies . . . . If your seats are in the first six rows in any theatre you'll feel quite comfortable and more festive if you are dressed." By "dressed" the Misses Josephy and McBride did not mean merely covering your naughty bits, but black tie for gentlemen and long dresses for ladies. In the Deco years, not only was this the only proper way to be attired for the theater, but if you were not "dressed" you were not passing through the pearly gates of clubs like El Morocco.

Elmo was the preferred roost of two night owls who were among its most important assets. Jerome Zerbe was a young photographer from Cleveland, Ohio, whom Perona hired in 1933 for

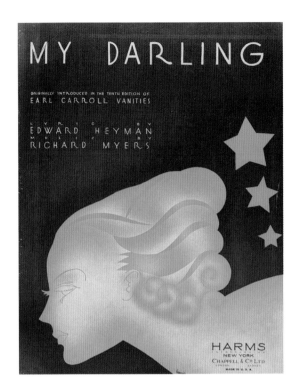

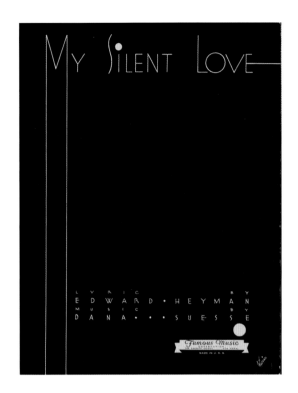

ABOVE LEFT AND RIGHT Both of these 1932 sheet music covers have an inescapably Deco look, in the one exemplified by the modeling of the woman's head and in the other by the sleekly modernistic sans-serif lettering. (Private Collection)

LEFT Sheet music cover for Sigmund Romberg's wildly successful 1926 operetta *The Desert Song*, with lyrics by Oscar Hammerstein II and Otto Harbach. The design consciously suggests the North African exoticism popularized by Rudolph Valentino in films such as 1921's *The Sheik*. (Private Collection)

$75 a week to take snaps of the club's patrons. Charming, intelligent, and socially well connected, Zerbe was deftly adept with the flash and soon El Morocco's cavorting denizens were appearing in magazines and newspapers from the Atlantic to the Pacific. The club's other priceless biped asset was Lucius Beebe. Considered by many to be New York's best-dressed man, Beebe, who had the distinction of having been an undergrad at both Harvard and Yale, sported a diamond gardenia on his satin lapel and was the society columnist of the city's most revered newspaper, the *Herald Tribune*. He was also a witty writer with a gift for clever metaphor. He coined the word "orchidaceous" to describe beautiful girls and once characterized a bottle of particularly awful wine as "Strictly Hackensack Meadows! Private Cuvée, 1921." Beebe understood fully the transformation that had been wrought on New York Society. In his picaresque chronicle *Snoot If You Must*, he observed: "The café society of New York was infinitely more democratic, more open to achievement, than the older social order. The requirements for membership in it were primarily those of professional success, personal distinction, and willingness to subscribe to only the vaguest of formal codes. Almost anybody with something to offer stood an excellent chance of becoming somebody in café society."

Just how democratic it was could be rapidly surmised by a quick glance at Elmo's dance floor where two orchestras played from dinner to dawn. There, as every cognizant Gothamite knew, to quote the immortal words of Cole Porter: "The crowds at El Morocco punish the parquet." The heady social bouillabaisse might include certified 24-carat socialites like top polo player Tommy Hitchcock and multimillionaire financier and movie producer John Hay "Jock" Whitney; peripatetic royalty like Grand Duchess Marie, first cousin of the last Czar; glamorous theater types like Moss Hart and Tallulah Bankhead; denizens of the demimonde, such as Jimmy Donahue, a Woolworth scion; beautiful women who had married their way to the top such as Mrs. Harrison (Mona) Williams, daughter of a Louisville horse trainer or groom, take your choice, who reputedly spent $150,000 a year to keep threads on her beautiful back; and, of course, Henry Luce and Clare Boothe Brokaw Luce.

The décor of El Morocco was unquestionably proto-Deco. When in 1932, interior decorator Vernon McFarlane was commissioned to transform a nondescript store into an exciting nightclub, it was not mere chance which led him to turn to one of France's North African colonies for inspiration. McFarlane was motivated by the same impulse which had driven French Art Deco designers to look to the Middle East, Southeast Asia, and Africa for design ideas. The visitor to El Morocco was greeted with "*Bon soir, m'sieu, madame*," by a doorman attired in the blue uniform of the French Foreign Legion, while inside, beneath an azure sky set with twinkling stars, the sense of a Saharan oasis was suggested by groves of artificial palm trees lining the walls and banquettes upholstered in boldly striped fake zebra skin. El Morocco might not have all the elements of a hotel bar in Marrakesh, but that was most definitely its intention.

If Brooks Atkinson spotted a paradox in the vitality of the Broadway theater in the midst of the hard economic realities of the 1930s, another striking paradox of the decade was America's

TOP The Silver Sandal Club in the 1939 musical *Swing Time*, starring Fred Astaire and Ginger Rogers, is a prime example of the reality of the New York nightclub being transferred to the fantasy world of the cinema. (Private Collection.)

BOTTOM The coming of the big bands in the mid-1930s led to the construction of enormous venues where New Yorkers could dance to the latest swing and Latin rhythms. One of the largest was the streamlined International Casino, Broadway and 44th Street, designed by Thomas W. Lamb and Donald Deskey. Completed in 1937, the complex, with its bar, cocktail lounge, restaurant, and dance floor, held more than 2,000. The music was often South American in flavor, featuring dances such as the wildly popular Conga. The chorus girls of the International Casino, with their slim silhouettes and glistening cellophane costumes, perfectly express the Deco age. (Museum of the City of New York.)

insatiable appetite for tidbits concerning the doings of New York café society, ranging from the breathtaking number of parties Noël Coward attended during his annual 12-week residence in the city to the price tag of "bringing out" debutants Cobina Wright and Brenda Frazier. In the very depths of the Depression Beebe was regaling readers with details of Mona Williams's new jewels and Winchell was informing Mr. and Mrs. North America that in Gotham the "ropes are up at the better cabarets—and the crowds bruise one another attempting to crash the gate." Almost all agreed that reading about the antics of café society in the newspapers was a welcome—and harmless—bit of escapism.

Curiously, New York's nightclub glamour would have its full apotheosis on the silver screen, to the accompaniment of matchless words and music. One of the prime inspirations for this phenomenon was New York's supreme Art Deco club created in 1931 by the Viennese-born architect and set designer, Joseph Urban. Located at 128 East 58th Street, the Park Avenue Restaurant, as it was called, boasted black walls with no decoration except three bold, white speed lines, a green ceiling, and a spectacular circular chrome and silver bar set into a niche sheathed with tall, vertical strips of mirror. The mirrors, which gave to the club a brilliant, brittle dazzle, allowed patrons facing the bar to see who was descending the cantilevered staircase, adorned with gilded metallic railings modeled on those of an ocean liner. The club's backers, a syndicate of some of New York's most notorious racketeers, paid Urban $50,000 in cash for the job. The glorious

Park Avenue Restaurant and its sensational bar were smashed to bits by federal agents in 1933 just before Repeal went into effect.

But Urban's Park Avenue club would have a life after life, becoming the model for Hollywood's supreme Art Deco nightclub, the Silver Sandal in RKO's 1936 masterpiece, *Swing Time*. That club, which appears to float magically above New York's skyscrapers, was the creation of John Harkrider, a New Yorker who had designed costumes for Florenz Ziegfeld. With its dramatic cantilevered double stairway, insistent black-and-white color scheme, glistening cellophane tablecloths, and shiny touches of chrome, the Silver Sandal whisked Park Avenue to the big screen. The transition is not surprising, for the film's writers and its lyricist, Dorothy Fields, were habitués of Gotham nightlife. When Georges Metaxa, the bandleader in *Swing Time*, announces to the gorgeously attired throng, "Everybody's here!" he clearly echoes Beebe and Winchell. And when the platinum blond Ginger Rogers, in a luminescent white gown with glittering rhinestone straps and a swaying skirt of tulle, steps out onto the reflecting onyxlike dance floor with Fred Astaire to the insistent rhythm of Jerome Kern's mesmerizing "Never Gonna Dance," all the sophisticated Art Deco ambience of New York 1930s nightlife is dazzlingly revealed and, fortunately, captured forever.

That intoxicating East Coast ambience owes not a little to Jerome Kern, who composed the memorable melodies—"Pick Yourself Up," "The Way You Look Tonight," and "A Fine Romance," in addition to "Never Gonna Dance"—which gave *Swing Time* much of its scintillating New York atmosphere. The composer was, in fact, a true New Yorker. He was born in the city in 1885, lived there or in nearby Bronxville most of his life, and died in Manhattan in 1945. It would be in New York, too, that his incandescent musicals, such as *Sally* of 1920 with "Look for the Silver Lining"; *Sunny* of 1925 with "Who?"; and *Show Boat* of 1927 which introduced, among other unforgettable songs, "Ol' Man River," "Make Believe," and "Bill" were presented. It is worth noting that while Kern was writing "Never Gonna Dance" for Fred and Ginger's cinematographically historic scene in the very New Yorkish Art Deco Silver Sandal, he was living in the Beverly Wilshire in a penthouse which he described with insouciant New York dismissiveness as "vulgar" and "hideously overdone."

NEWS
ATRE
E of
HILD
ASTOR THEATRE
George ARLISS
in The HOUSE of ROTHSCHILD
GAIETY
JACK HOLT
END OF THE WORLD
THE SCREENS MOST
DARING SPECTACLE
END of the WORLD
NOT FOR CHILDREN
25¢
PALACE
THE HOUSE
ROTHSCHILD
108 JERSEY CITY NEWARK

# SKYSCRAPERS

The Art Deco era was the last when the raw power of engineering was reined in by design. The modernist mantra attributed to Mies van der Rohe that "less is more" gave to every real estate developer, in the years following the Second World War, the moral justification to aesthetically short-change the public. A vivid illustration of the continental divide separating the structures built in New York before and after 1940 is unfolded every time one flies over Manhattan in the evening. Peering through the airplane's windows at the fabulous Canaan below, passengers invariably exclaim: "There's the Chrysler Building!" "That's the Empire State!" One never hears "There's the Pan Am" (now the Met Life), though Walter Gropius's elephantine 2.4-million-square-foot 1960s concrete tombstone is far larger than the buildings which are greeted with delight. In *Will They Ever Finish Bruckner Boulevard?* published in 1963, the doyenne of New York's architectural critics, Ada Louise Huxtable, intrepidly set forth one reason why the Pan Am and its ilk are such civically devastating fiascoes: "A $100 million building cannot really be called cheap. But Pan-Am is a colossal collection of minimums. Its exterior and its public spaces, in particular, use minimum good materials of minimum acceptable quality executed with a minimum of imagination (always an expensive commodity), or distinction (which comes high), or finesse (which costs more). Pan-Am is gigantically second-rate."

One of the essential elements—an element too readily overlooked or dismissed—which draws the viewer to Art Deco skyscrapers like the Chrysler Building and is missing from structures such as the Pan Am is visual zest, enthusiasm, *joie de vivre.* This element, this quality, informing Deco architecture is marvelously delineated by Claude Bragdon, who brought to his architectural criticism the spiritual insights of Theosophy, as well as the pictorial awareness of his career as a set designer

ABOVE The Barclay-Vesey Building, begun in 1923, is considered by many to be New York's first Art Deco skyscraper. The work of the firm of McKenzie, Voorhees & Gmelin, with the architect Ralph Walker in charge, the building, constructed to provide offices and a switching center for the New York Telephone Company, was instantly praised for its imaginative cubistic massing and its uncompromising verticality. (The Metropolitan Museum of Art.)

OPPOSITE The treatment of the rooftop silhouette of the Barclay-Vesey Building on West Street between Barclay and Vesey streets presented a notable change on the New York skyline. Here was no Greek temple nor Venetian campanile, but a series of massive piers which expressed dynamic modernity. Ralph Walker said of his structure that it was a building that "looks but little to the past, much to the present, and therefore tries to glimpse the future." (Historic Architecture Collection, The Art Institute of Chicago.)

and the discipline of his training as an architect. In *The Frozen Fountain* of 1932, Bragdon described skyscrapers as though they were geysers, springs, and fountains scattered over New York's landscape:

> A building a fountain: how clarifying a point of view! I have only to look out of my window at those upthrust acres of steel, brick, and concrete which hide the river, laten the sunrise, shadow the streets, and diminish the sky. . . . The needle-pointed *flèche* of the Chrysler tower catches the sunlight like a fountain's highest expiring jet. The set-backs of the broad and massive lofts and industrials appear now in the semblance of cascades descending in successive stages from the summits to which they have been upthrust. The white vertical masses of the Waldorf-Astoria, topped with silver, seem a plexus of upward gushing fountains, most powerful and therefore highest at the center, descending by ordered stages to the broad Park Avenue river.

OPPOSITE The lobby of the Barclay-Vesey Building has a ceiling decorated with ten murals by Mack, Jenney & Tyler telling the story of communications from Babylon's clay tablets to contemporary radio broadcasting. The Deco bronze and glass chandeliers suggested the shape of the building itself. (Historic Architecture Collection, The Art Institute of Chicago.)

Bragdon concludes his book by looking beyond steel and stone and commanding architects to "wake up and dream."

"Dream" is a word entirely alien to the vocabulary of the International Style, which was the theoretical foundation of buildings like the Pan Am. Indeed, in his "The Theory and Organization of the Bauhaus," written in 1922, Walter Gropius flaunts its dreamless aesthetics: "We want to create a clear, organic architecture, whose inner logic will be radiant and naked, unencumbered by lying façades and trickeries." While it is true that there are Bauhaus-inspired structures of merit in New York—Skidmore, Owings & Merrill's Pepsi-Cola Building at 500 Park Avenue of 1960 and their Manufacturers Trust Company offices of 1954 at 510 Fifth Avenue among them—the list is woefully short.

New York's Art Deco monuments of the late 1920s and early 1930s have in the past more often than not been included among those edifices presenting "lying façades and trickeries." The architect Philip Johnson savagely attacked the Art Deco skyscrapers for their "dishonesty," and even an architectural historian as distinguished as James Marston Fitch passed them by with scarcely a nod of recognition. In his *American Building: The Historical Forces That Shaped It* of 1947, Fitch writes: "At first glance, the period from 1900 to 1933 appears to be an aesthetic wasteland: and a closer scrutiny of the individual buildings of the period does little to correct that first impression." After admitting that there was "a certain bleak majesty in the scale of the skylines rising all over America," Fitch grudgingly takes note of Raymond Hood's Daily News and McGraw-Hill buildings because "they depend chiefly upon simplification for effect."

Simplicity is not one of the supreme characteristics of design. In 1966, with his *Complexity and Contradiction in Architecture*, published, curiously enough, by the Museum of Modern Art, Robert Venturi dealt a deadly blow to those architects who had made "less" and "simple" their *sine qua non*: "Orthodox Modern architects have tended to recognize complexity insufficiently or inconsistently. In their attempt to break with tradition and start all over again, they idealized the primitive and elementary at the expense of the diverse and sophisticated." Thus Mies van

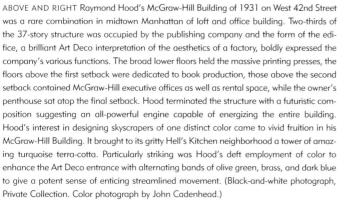

ABOVE AND RIGHT Raymond Hood's McGraw-Hill Building of 1931 on West 42nd Street was a rare combination in midtown Manhattan of loft and office building. Two-thirds of the 37-story structure was occupied by the publishing company and the form of the edifice, a brilliant Art Deco interpretation of the aesthetics of a factory, boldly expressed the company's various functions. The broad lower floors held the massive printing presses, the floors above the first setback were dedicated to book production, those above the second setback contained McGraw-Hill executive offices as well as rental space, while the owner's penthouse sat atop the final setback. Hood terminated the structure with a futuristic composition suggesting an all-powerful engine capable of energizing the entire building. Hood's interest in designing skyscrapers of one distinct color came to vivid fruition in his McGraw-Hill Building. It brought to its gritty Hell's Kitchen neighborhood a tower of amazing turquoise terra-cotta. Particularly striking was Hood's deft employment of color to enhance the Art Deco entrance with alternating bands of olive green, brass, and dark blue to give a potent sense of enticing streamlined movement. (Black-and-white photograph, Private Collection. Color photograph by John Cadenhead.)

OPPOSITE A building very different from that of the McGraw-Hill was designed in 1926 by Joseph Urban for the publisher William Randolph Hearst. Drawing inspiration from the Viennese work of his hero, Otto Wagner, Urban crafted on 8th Avenue between 56th and 57th streets an eye-catching home for Hearst's magazines, seen here at the left. Truly imperial, the International Magazine Building reflected the larger-than-life personality of its owner. High fluted columns topped with urns typical of those found at the 1925 Paris Exposition rose from the building's four corners and in the center of its façades. At the base of each column Art Deco statues by Henry Kheis symbolized subjects relating to the magazine business, including Sport, Industry, Music, and Printing. Though the edifice was only six stories high when completed in 1928, it was constructed so that floors could be added as needed. A glass and metal tower, which contrasts sharply with Urban's design, now rises above the original structure. (Private Collection.)

der Rohe in 1922 could disseminate the theory that "Skyscrapers reveal their bold structural pattern during construction. Only then does the gigantic steel web seem impressive. When the outer walls are put in place, the structural system which is the basis of all artistic design, is hidden by a chaos of meaningless and trivial forms." Added to the Viennese architect and moralist Adolph Loos's pronouncement that architecture should be divorced from art, that decoration is, in fact, sin, one has the theoretical underpinnings for the dehumanizing edifices of stark white brick, blank metal panels, and lifeless glass walls which have shot up across New York since the 1950s.

The architects of New York's Art Deco skyscrapers had been inoculated against this minimalist plague by the still-potent power of the École des Beaux-Arts. An astonishing number had attended the school on Paris's Left Bank, among them Raymond Hood, Ely Jacques Kahn, Harvey Wiley Corbett, Wallace K. Harrison, and William Van Alen. All had heard reiterated time and again the École's first and greatest commandment that the basis of architectural perfection was the classical tradition of ancient Greece and Rome as exemplified by the five orders—Tuscan, Doric, Ionic, Corinthian, and Composite. Through the study of the orders—their correct height, diameter, and intercolumniation—and an analysis of the other elements of ancient buildings an architect was prepared to take his first steps toward designing a structure which would possess those essential qualities enunciated in the 16th century by the Italian architect Andrea Palladio in *The Four Books of Architecture:* "utility or convenience, duration and beauty." But the École's objective was not to train architects who would cover the face of the earth with replicas of Athens'

Parthenon or Rome's Pantheon, but rather architects who would employ its dictates to construct contemporary edifices imbued with harmony, pleasing proportions, appropriate decoration, and with a plan which fit perfectly the building's purpose. Indeed, the École's most popular lecture course was the one on new materials and building methods. Thus the future Art Deco architects who matriculated at the École were like the young Pablo Picasso whose academic training in drawing from life at Barcelona's Royal Academy of Art was the ground from which he could take flight into daring experimentation. The informing lessons of the École are especially evident in New York's Art Deco skyscrapers which dot Manhattan Island from the elegant undulating limestone elevations of Voorhees, Gmelin & Walker's Irving Trust Company (now the Bank of New York) of 1929–1931 at One Wall Street to the brilliantly proportioned massing of Ely Jacques Kahn's snowy marble Squibb Building of 1930 at the southeast corner of Fifth Avenue and 58th Street.

The very existence of the skyscraper is a graphic example of form following function. Though George B. Post had, in 1881, with his Produce Exchange on Bowling Green, begun experimenting with construction which combined metal framing and masonry, it was left to William Le Baron Jenney with his Home Insurance Building of 1884 in Chicago to construct the world's first completely iron-and-steel framed structure. The 10-story edifice whose outer walls were not load-bearing, but merely thin curtains attached to the metal frame, proved that there were almost no practical limits to a building's height. New York's first all-metal framed edifice was Bradford L. Gilbert's Tower Building of 1888 at 50 Broadway. It was a mere 11 stories, but city officials vigorously questioned the safety, as they said, of "standing a steel bridge structure on end." To publicize his building's stability Gilbert himself occupied the two top floors. New York soon had other metal-framed high-rises, including George Post's 16-story Pulitzer Building on Park Row, completed in 1890. Its extraordinary height led one wag, when he stepped off the elevator on the top floor, to quip, "Is God in?" These new buildings soon had a label, "skyscraper," a term adapted from the name of the top sail crowning a tall ship.

The form of the skyscraper was the result of a confluence of a number of spectacular industrial and scientific breakthroughs: the availability of high-grade iron and later of steel; Elisha Otis's perfection of the elevator, first demonstrated in New York in the 1850s; steam heat; Thomas Alva Edison's incandescent bulb of 1879; and Alexander Graham Bell's telephone, given its first public demonstration in 1876. Behind the form of this new building type was the economic reality which made it financially viable. By the 1880s, with the economic dislocations of the Civil War and Reconstruction rapidly disappearing, the American economy began to boom. Thousands of miles of new rail lines were laid and alongside of them telegraph wires were strung linking the vast, now undivided, Union. New corporations, including Standard Oil and American Tobacco and Pullman and I. M. Singer and Woolworth and Metropolitan Life Insurance, needed gigantic structures to house their growing armies of office workers who were responsible for bookkeeping, inventory recording, supervising sales agents, and overseeing legal matters. With the railroads stretching from coast to coast and from Canada to the Gulf and

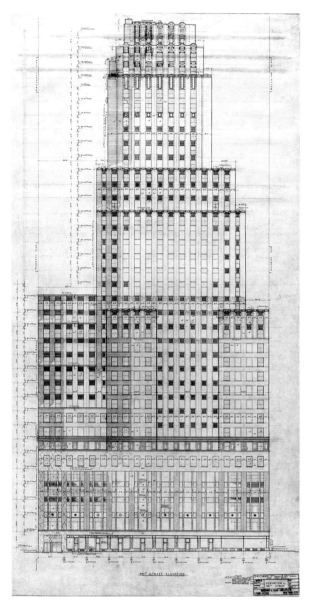

The 56th Street elevation of Ely Jacques Kahn's Squibb Building. (Avery Architectural and Fine Arts Library, Columbia University.)

The Squibb Building was completed in 1931. This geometric glory in white marble, white glazed brick, and white terra-cotta was the architect's favorite building. McKim, Mead & White's Savoy-Plaza is to the left. (Library of Congress.)

with the telegraph and telephone reaching into every town and village, it was suddenly possible to concentrate these multifarious operations at a single site. Corporate headquarters were soon clustered in Chicago, Pittsburgh, Hartford, Philadelphia, and, above all, in New York. A major factor in Gotham's primacy was its matchless array of investment banks: J. P. Morgan, the Rockefellers' National City Bank, Kuhn Loeb, the U.S. Trust, and the Bank of New York, to name but a few. In the 1890s, the French novelist Paul Bourget, gazing upon the recently completed skyscrapers housing America's corporations, proclaimed that they were "the first draught of a new sort of art." New York's Art Deco skyscrapers would carry that art to perfection.

The tall building, though, was not without its detractors. They drew their arguments from two sources. The first was America's bucolic tradition whose patron saint was Thomas Jefferson. In his *Notes on the State of Virginia* of 1784, Jefferson had unequivocally stated that "The mobs of great cities add just so much to the support of pure government, as sores do to the strength of the human body." This view got a boost from Ralph Waldo Emerson, who maintained that "The intellect may be kept clean and healthful if man will live the life of nature." These sentiments are the heart of the Garden City movement of the 19th century which quaintly equated residential heaven with white picket fences and rambling roses. Undoubtedly this was behind the macabre 1926 proposal of Thomas Hastings—who with John Carrère had

ABOVE LEFT At the Beaux-Arts Ball held at the Hotel Astor on January 23, 1931, several of New York's leading architects wore costumes based on buildings they had designed. From left to right: A. Stewart Walker as the Fuller Building; Leonard Schultze as the Waldorf-Astoria; Ely Jacques Kahn as the Squibb Building; William Van Alen as the Chrysler Building; Ralph Walker as the Irving Trust Company; and Joseph Freedlander as the Museum of the City of New York. (Avery Architectural and Fine Arts Library, Columbia University.)

ABOVE RIGHT The Irving Trust (now the Bank of New York) at the southeast corner of Broadway and Wall Street, completed in 1932 from designs by Ralph Walker of Voorhees, Gmelin & Walker, is a limestone masterpiece of Art Deco design. (The Bank of New York Archives.)

ABOVE LEFT The French Renaissance Singer Building, Broadway and Liberty Street, was constructed in stages between 1897 and 1908 from designs by Ernest Flagg. The 612-foot-tall edifice was typical of the towers springing up in New York to hold the burgeoning office staffs of America's expanding corporations. Singer manufactured sewing machines. (Private Collection.)

RIGHT The General Electric Building—originally the RCA Victor Building—at the southwest corner of Lexington and 51st Street has a Deco crown with touches of Gothic whose exuberant details represented the electricity which powered the Victor talking machines. (Historic Architecture Collection, The Art Institute of Chicago.)

created the dazzling New York Public Library at Fifth Avenue and 42nd Street—that no structure taller than eight stories should be built in Gotham.

The second source of animosity toward the skyscraper was aimed not so much at its form as at its function: providing offices for big business. Typically, the anticapitalist University of Chicago economist Thorstein Veblen, in articles and books such as *The Theory of the Leisure Class*, excoriated the skyscraper as one of the supreme symbols of a grasping capitalism. Both the bucolic and the anticapitalist strains found a particularly powerful voice in the critic and urban theorist, Lewis Mumford. In an article "Is the Skyscraper Tolerable?" of 1927, Mumford made his anticapitalist point of view inescapably apparent when he stated bluntly that the skyscraper's one purpose was to crowd more people into the city and "bring a congested use to the land, which automatically increased the economic rent." It is significant that, in the 1930s, while serving as the architecture critic of the *New Yorker*, Mumford should forsake New York's urban thicket for a farmhouse in pastoral Dutchess County.

There was, though, it must be admitted, a potential problem with these new buildings which

Cross & Cross, the architects who designed the RCA Victor Building—now the General Electric Building—made the lobby a tunnel of modernity, with an aluminum leaf ceiling, which fit perfectly the very up-to-the-moment product RCA sold. (Photograph by Kevin Downs.)

The Graybar Building's name derives from Gray and Barton, the Cleveland-based electrical manufacturing company which became the Western Electric Manufacturing Company. Western Electric made Alexander Graham Bell's first telephone. While Western Electric continued to make products exclusively for Bell, in 1926 its distribution of electric products for other customers was reorganized under the name Graybar. When Sloan & Robertson completed its massive cubistic building at 420 Lexington Avenue in 1927, Graybar was doing more than 75 million dollars in business annually. Appropriately, the architects placed above the building's entrances heroic bas-relief figures symbolizing electricity and power. (Museum of the City of New York.)

While the 56-story Chanin Building of 1929 at the southwest corner of Lexington Avenue and 42nd Street pales in comparison externally with its exuberant neighbor the Chrysler building, inside it is a very different story. Here the infatuation of the brilliant real estate developer Irwin Chanin with Art Deco is given free rein. Working with René Chambellan, Chanin created a lobby that is a fugue of geometry centered on the theme of the "City of Opportunity" depicted by fantasy skylines in the bronze reliefs over the principal doorways. The entrance gates by Chambellan and Jacques Delamarre leading to Mr. Chanin's office on the 52nd floor are a dramatic depiction of the philosophic underpinnings of Art Deco: industry—symbolized by wheels and gears—and the rewards of industry—wealth, symbolized by the stacks of coins at the bottom of the gates. (All three images: Private Collection.)

stretched endlessly skyward, creating a vast vertical city. The result, in the words of Mumford, could be "unheard of degrees of congestion." One attempt to ameliorate the problem would profoundly affect the form of the Art Deco skyscraper. It is significant that William Le Baron Jenney's revolutionary iron-and-steel framed office building should have been built for an insurance company, for in the boom years of the Gilded Age no category of corporation expanded more quickly than did those selling insurance. In 1912, the Equitable Life Assurance Society began constructing a new headquarters in lower Manhattan on a one-acre lot bounded by Broadway, Nassau, Pine, and Cedar streets. The architect was Ernest R. Graham of the Chicago firm of Graham, Anderson, Probst & White. By the time it was completed in 1915, the bulky 40-story Equitable filled its entire site with an astounding 1.2 million square feet of office space into which were packed 15,000 workers. "The building robs us of sunlight and sky," a vestryman of nearby Trinity Church complained, while the owners of the graceful Singer Tower across Broadway announced that the proximity of the Equitable Building adversely affected the value of their property.

As a result of the egregious example of the Equitable, in 1916 New York became the first city in the United States to pass a zoning ordinance. Under it, a building's permitted height from the pavement was to be calculated by multiples of the width of the street it faced. Above 300 feet, all buildings, in order to preserve light and air for neighboring structures and pedestrians, were required to have setbacks. The aesthetic consequences of the 1916 zoning ordinance would be fully revealed in the building boom of the late 1920s and early 1930s. To make the most of the site, builders and architects would push to the very edge of the public pavement, a standard device of every Art Deco skyscraper, and the required setbacks would be given cubistic volume which fit perfectly into the Art Deco canon.

It would be a mistake to leave the impression that all architects, all city planners, all critics recoiled from the explosive growth, the concentration of population, the perturbation of New York. The growth had certainly been spectacular: from 1 million in 1860, to $3\frac{1}{2}$ million in 1900, to nearly 5 million in 1920. In an article published in the *Palette Knife* in 1931, the well-known art critic Henry McBride wittily answered the nay-sayers, including the well-known architectual critic Lewis Mumford:

> I like life enormously as it is, particularly as it is lived in New York. The congestion that so disturbs Mr.
> Mumford seems much to the taste of average New Yorkers. They particularly like to go where they think
> everybody is going and if a percentage of them get killed in the effort to see Mr. Babe Ruth play baseball,
> why it is apt to be considered a more than usually successful afternoon. As for the looks of the place, that
> suits me too. Of course it is archaic. But it has a wild and curious beauty.

But it was left to the incomparable lyricist and composer Cole Porter, who had skipped out from the small town of Peru, Indiana, for the incandescences of the big city, to write the ultimate Manhattan ballad. The song appeared in Porter's 1930 musical, *The New Yorkers*, and was appropriately named "I Happen to Like New York." It included these lines:

*I like the city air, I like to drink of it,*
*The more I know New York, the more I think of it.*
*I like the sight and the sound and even the stink of it.*

The true foundation for the acceptance of, or, better, the enthusiasm for, the dense urbanity of New York, symbolized by the skyscraper, was the opportunity offered by city life. If the Statue of Liberty promised a better existence for the immigrants coming to America from Europe, the skyscraper, particularly in its Art Deco guise, promised a better existence to both native New Yorkers and to those migrating to the metropolis from America's rural hinterlands. The yearning for rustication felt by world-weary urban sophisticates scurrying to the boondocks of New York State, New Jersey, and Connecticut was not shared by the men and women of the 1920s and 30s whose parents had been maids and janitors in Gotham or farmers and day laborers in small town and rural America. They would have undoubtedly agreed with the Italian Futurist Marinetti, who preferred "the 'vroom' of an engine to the Victory of Samothrace." Their thoughts and fears are perfectly expressed by Carol Kennicott when she first glimpses her new husband's Minnesota hometown in Sinclair Lewis's iconographic 1920 novel, *Main Street:* "And she saw that Gopher Prairie was merely an enlargement of all the hamlets which they had been passing. . . . The huddled low wooden houses broke the plains scarcely more than would a hazel thicket. The fields swept up to it, past it. It was unprotected and unprotecting; there was no dignity in it nor any hope of greatness."

By 1930 almost half the people in the United States lived within a radius of 20 to 50 miles of a city with a population of more than 100,000. The expanding corporations like General Electric and Chrysler and Bell Telephone and new businesses like public relations, advertising, cosmetics, radio, and newsreel production needed ever more office workers and provided entry-level jobs for men and women as secretaries, researchers, file clerks, and mailroom employees. Compared to cooking and polishing silver in the homes of the rich or baling hay and cutting corn on the prairies of the Midwest, these jobs promised opportunity, excitement, and freedom. This sense that the new world of the 1920s and 1930s, the world of the fast car, the fast elevator, the fast train, was incontestable proof of the progress of mankind conformed perfectly with the optimism which was a cornerstone of Art Deco architecture. Just as the stained glass windows and the sculpture of the medieval cathedral were there to instruct the worshiper in the fundamentals of his faith, the art and ornament of the Deco skyscraper sought to promulgate to New Yorkers the idea that they were living in a world better than that of their fathers. The theme, significantly, for all of the art embellishing Rockefeller Center was "New Frontiers and the March of Civilization," and the bronze frieze by René Chambellan and Jacques Delamarre on the base of Sloan & Robertson's Chanin Building blazoned forth the story of evolution. The kinetic spirit of New York on the brink of the Deco decades is graphically described by Anita Loos in her

New York in the 1920s and 1930s was the focus of American newsreel production. To house this new and booming business Ely Jacques Kahn designed on Ninth Avenue between 44th and 45th streets the Film Center Building, which was completed in 1929. Though Kahn was beginning to abandon color on the exterior of his buildings, as evident at 120 Wall Street, this was most certainly not true of his lobbies. At the Film Center he employed pink, black, and white marble, as well as blue and orange terra-cotta, to create an appropriately jazzy entrance to this skyscraper of creativity.

TOP RIGHT Decorative metalwork over the entrance of the Film Center Building. (Photograph by John Cadenhead.)

ABOVE AND BOTTOM RIGHT Two views of the Film Center's lobby. Kahn lavishly employed gold on the upper walls and ceiling of the lobby to give a sense of opulence to a structure which was, essentially, a loft building. The ceiling, with its broken surfaces and dramatic variation in the planes, carries the skewed perspectives of Cubist painting into the realm of architecture. (Photographs by John Cadenhead.)

memoir, *A Girl Like I*. Arriving from the West Coast on the *Twentieth Century Limited* in 1920, the future author of *Gentlemen Prefer Blondes* quickly perceived that she had entered a world very different from the one she had left behind: "I walked the length of Grand Central Station, through swarms of people who looked as if they were hurrying toward some exciting goal; there was none of the lethargy of Southern California where nobody seemed to have a destination worth getting to."

The lobbies of the Deco skyscrapers are the narthexes of the new cathedrals of commerce. Crafted with the care which Viennese and French designers like Josef Hoffman and Jean Dunand lavished on their furniture, they present a dramatic contrast to postwar lobbies whose bleakness is feebly disguised by forests of ficus and whose omnipresent gray metal elevator doors suggest the crematorium. William Van Alen's Chrysler Building lobby is the quintessential expression of

The Chrysler Building, Lexington Avenue between 42nd and 43rd streets, is the monument of William Van Alen who studied at Brooklyn's Pratt Institute, worked for a number of architects, including Clinton & Russell, and became a partner of H. Craig Severance. The client, Walter P. Chrysler, insisted that the 68-story skyscraper's decorative scheme celebrate the automobile. A frieze of Chrysler hubcaps embellished the 30th floor, while the voids below the spire suggested the spokes of a wheel. ABOVE RIGHT: Chrysler building under construction. (Photograph by Walker Evans Canadian Centre for Architecture, Montreal.) ABOVE LEFT: Elevator doors in the lobby of the Chrysler Building. (Private Collection.)

ABOVE LEFT On the 61st floor gargoyles in the form of chromium nickel-steel Deco eagles guard the Chrysler tower. (Photograph by Margaret Bourke White, Canadian Centre for Architecture, Montreal.)

ABOVE RIGHT Architect Van Alen supplied drama to the three-story-high black marble Lexington Avenue entrance of the Chrysler Building by making it appear that the structure's walls were parting to permit entrance to its lobby. (Photograph by John Cadenhead.)

OPPOSITE The 77-story Chrysler Building at the northeast corner of Lexington Avenue and 42nd Street designed by William Van Alen and built between 1928 and 1930 exemplifies the aesthetic power of Art Deco. Though the Empire State soon surpassed it in height, the Chrysler's stainless steel spire with its triangular openings remains one of Manhattan's most stirring aesthetic experiences. Constructed of black, white, and gray brick, the structure has numerous visual references to the company of its owner, Walter P. Chrysler. Among them are the stylized winged radiator caps on the 30th floor, one of which may be seen in this photograph. (Photograph by John Cadenhead.)

Though the tower of the Empire State Building was designed to be a mooring mast, it was used only twice. In this photograph, taken in December of 1930, the zeppelin *U.S. Los Angeles* is seen approaching the building, but the coupling did not take place. (Private Collection.)

the genre. Entering from the Lexington Avenue side one passes through a doorway which is, in fact, a three-story parted black marble curtain, a modern reminiscence of the carved stone draperies found in South German Baroque churches. The drama of the Baroque continues inside where the unexpected triangular shape of the lobby embodies the Deco love of movement, while the senses are assaulted by a sensational use of rich and exotic materials: a yellow Siena marble floor, walls of red North African marble, with, here and there, touches of precious onyx and blue marble and bands of silver. Unlike International Style architects who, when it comes to ceilings, suffer aesthetic amnesia, Van Alen caps his lobby with Edward Trumbull's mural *Energy, Result, Workmanship and Transportation,* with its perspective-bending view of the Chrysler Building itself.

Appropriately, the lobby's ornamental finale is its elevator doors, ceremonial portals to the offices above. Their extravagant veneers of satinwood, walnut, Japanese ash, and curly maple recall the luxurious boiseries of the pavilions of the 1925 Paris Exposition. Their fan motif—most likely inspired by the fans carried by the servants accompanying the Egyptian pharaoh Tutankhamen on the dazzling painted box found in his tomb in 1922—is an unforgettable example of the Deco style's success in finding design sources beyond the European tradition.

The climax of the Deco skyscraper was undoubtedly the Empire State Building by Shreve, Lamb & Harmon at the southwest corner of Fifth Avenue and 34th Street. Begun in 1929 during the stock market boom, it was completed in 1931 in the Depression. The limestone structure's elegant, urbane massing and its unbroken stripes of windows with aluminum spandrels and frames of nickel chrome steel evince a sense of soaring like that of no other skyscraper. The Empire State is topped by a 200-foot-tall aluminum, chrome-nickel steel, and glass finial embraced by wings.

The concept of the office as a place of glamour and liberation for men and also, it should be emphasized, for women, was effectively disseminated by the cinema. The enormous power of this medium may be seen from the statistics given by Donald Albrecht in *Designing Dreams: Modern Architecture and the Movies:* "By 1939, weekly attendance at America's 17,000 movie houses was an astonishing 85,000,000." And almost inevitably the design of the offices in the new films was Art

The focus of the Empire State Building's three-story-high marble lobby was a representation of the building itself, with rays of sunlight emanating from the mooring mast atop it like beams of holiness radiating from the head of a saint. (Private Collection.)

The Fifth Avenue entrance of the Empire State Building. (Photograph by John Cadenhead.)

Deco. The Deco sets of the wonderfully named *Big Business Girl* of 1931, created by Jack Okey, were the perfect background for this tale of the ascension of a young woman from stenographer to advertising executive. And for the 1937 film *Artists and Models*, Hans Dreier and Kem Weber designed a Deco reception area whose curved glass-block desk and touches of chrome were the personification of thousands of offices in the Chrysler, Chanin, RCA, and other New York skyscrapers.

Critical curmudgeons, like Mumford, often with political agendas, continued to attack the tall office building, saying that in its very form it expressed "the dangers of plutocracy." In a 1931 article written on the occasion of the dedication of the Empire State, cultural critic Edmund Wilson found space both to revel in his perception that the Depression would mean the end of such towers and to ridicule some outstanding ones. Wilson began by skewering the Chrysler Building—"a tiny-scaled armadillo-tail ending in a stiff sting-like drill"—and went on to deplore "the white vertically-grooved and flat-headed Daily News Building, the Luna Park summits of the American Radiator Building, like a chocolate cake with gooey gilt icing."

Another view, a more lyrical and a more profound one, was offered by the poet, essayist, and storyteller, E. B. White. A lover of all aspects of Gotham, of its willow trees and skyscrapers, White in *Here Is New York,* published in 1949, precisely delineated what, spiritually and physically, the Olympian towers of the 1920s and 30s embodied:

> Manhattan has been compelled to expand skyward because of the absence of any other direction in which to grow. This, more than any other thing, is responsible for its physical majesty. It is to the nation what the white church spire is to the village—the visible symbol of aspiration and faith, the white plume saying that the way is up. The summer traveler swings in over Hell Gate Bridge and from the window of his sleeping car as it glides above the pigeon lofts and back yards of Queens looks southwest to where the morning light first strikes the steel peaks of midtown, and he sees its upward thrust unmistakable: the great walls and towers rising, the smoke rising, the heat not yet rising, the hopes and ferments of so many awakening millions rising—this vigorous spear that presses heaven hard.

# MODERN LIVING: RESIDENCES AND INSTITUTIONS

If one were to select the most authoritative voice for the taste of New York's upper and upper middle classes in the 1920s and 1930s, Mrs. Price Post, better known as Emily, would be it. A daughter of Bruce Price, the architect who planned the canonically correct community of Tuxedo Park, Mrs. Post never lost her inherited interest in architecture and design. In the mid-1920s she built an apartment house in accordance with her ideas of design at 39 East 79th Street. She chose the architects, planned the layouts, and raised the capital. Emily Post's iconic treatise on proper behavior, *Etiquette*, published in 1922, would, by 1950, have gone through 77 editions. While *Etiquette* is brimful of useful tips on "when to shake hands" and warnings about the use of such vulgar abbreviations as "phone, photo, and auto," there is also a chapter on "The Well-Appointed House," with appropriate alarms as to the social dangers of indifferently cleaned brass, coarse lace curtains, and golden oak.

In 1930 Mrs. Post assembled her thoughts on, among other things, painted furniture, beamed ceilings, and lambrequins in *The Personality of a House: The Blue Book of Home Design and Decoration*. The very first paragraph of the very first page sets forth the author's sentiments on these matters:

> Hundreds of textbooks have been written, covering every period of domestic architecture, interior ornamentation and furnishing, from oldest Egyptian antiquities to latest modern obliquities. But the personality of a house, the quality that appeals not merely to our critical faculties, but to our personal emotions, has been left out altogether—overlooked perhaps, or possibly taken for granted, as though a collection of valuable possessions must of themselves confer charm. And yet charm is precisely what the majority of houses lack.

Charm was the *sine qua non* of design for Mrs. Post and for the vast majority of well-off New Yorkers.

Some 490 pages later and after more than 60 illustrations of rooms furnished in American Colonial, Greek Revival, Spanish, Italian Renaissance, English Jacobean, and Georgian styles, Emily, gingerly, like a hiker poking a snake with a stick to ascertain whether or not it is dead, approaches "The Style We Know as Modern." She does not mask her distaste:

> The Moderns talk and write as though their revolution—their convention, their iconoclasm, their reconstruction, their return to the Stone Age, their claim of a new dimension—were as simple and as consistent as three plus three and two plus four. But to an onlooker—even a most interested onlooker—the contradictions of Modern design are more than confusing.

ABOVE Bols de violet daybed with gilt details, ca. 1929, Émile-Jacques Ruhlmann. This daybed, which could also serve as a sofa, is obviously inspired by the Empire style which flourished under Napoleon I. Ruhlmann's clients were drawn from the *gratin* of French society, for his exquisitely crafted pieces incorporating rare woods, lacquer, ivory, and bronze were costly. Indeed the price of a piece such as the one shown here was often more than the price of a middle-class house. His furnishings for the Hôtel d'un Collectionneur at the 1925 Paris Exposition would certainly have struck Emily Post as, if not "insane," at least quite macabre. (Courtesy Maison Gerard, Ltd.)

OPPOSITE The "cocktail room" of cosmetics czarina Elizabeth Arden's apartment at 834 Fifth Avenue which she purchased in the early 1930s. The avant-garde interior furnished with impressive Deco pieces was the creation of Nicolai Remisoff, who had been a set designer in Paris for Diaghilev's Ballets Russes. The exuberant painting is also by Remisoff. The presence of the horse is significant, for Miss Arden's Main Chance Farm was a powerhouse in the world of thoroughbred racing. (Historic Architecture Collection, The Art Institute of Chicago.)

Otto Wagner's apartment building of 1898, Linke Wienzeile #38, Vienna. The decorative medallions are by Koloman Moser. (Private Collection.)

As for the rooms and furniture of the 1925 Paris Exposition, they suggested "an insane copyist of William Morris who had just taken a dose of Paris green." Needless to say "revolution" and "iconoclasm" in any form were not welcome on Park and Fifth Avenues, or in Places such as Beekman and Sutton, or even in Murray Hill. And Mrs. Post, as was often the case, was right. The new, moderne style did have about it a whiff of Jacobinism.

The Viennese movement, organized in 1897–98, which is at the heart of so much modern design and is the first step toward Art Deco, proudly proclaimed itself the "Secession." What those who embraced the movement were seceding from was the staggering array of historical styles which had sprung up on Vienna's Ringstrasse, the broad boulevard created after 1858, when the Emperor Franz Joseph ordered the destruction of his capital's inner ramparts. Here in close proximity rose the twin-spired French Gothic Revival Votivkirche, the Flemish-style Rathaus or City Hall, the classical Greek Parliament Building, and the Italian Neo-Renaissance Opera House. Led by the great painter Gustav Klimt, the designer Koloman Moser, and the architects Otto Wagner, Joseph Olbrich, and Josef Hoffmann, the Secessionists drew upon sources as varied as the English and Scottish Arts and Crafts Movements and Art Nouveau to produce a Jugendstil, a new style liberated from historicism.

The Secessionists's premier architect, Otto Wagner (1841–1918), in his seminal 1895 textbook *Modern Architecture,* brilliantly presented the aesthetic conundrum faced by the Western world. In the past, Wagner wrote, each architectural style had developed naturally from the style preceding it. "New construction, new materials, new human tasks and views called forth a change or reconstitution of existing forms. Great social changes have always given birth to new styles." But in the last half of the 19th century, he notes, change came so swiftly that architects could not devise a style to express contemporary needs and outlooks and thus they went to their libraries to find past styles which might serve the purposes of the present. That was the meaning of the encyclopedic historical eclecticism found on the Ringstrasse and in the major cities of Europe and America. To counter this structural archeology, Wagner sets forth a creed which Mrs. Post would most certainly recognize as revolutionary: "The whole basis of the views of architecture prevailing today must be replaced by the recognition that the only possible point of departure for our artistic creation is modern life."

It was his determination to create dwellings that reflected modern life which led Wagner, who had been a traditionalist, to abandon the prevailing style of the Viennese apartment building. Known, appropriately, as *Wohnpalast,* an apartment palace, these four- to six-story structures attempted to conceal the fact that behind their common façade they contained on an average 16 units. With their rusticated ground floor and above that one or two floors set off by pilasters and other classical devices signaling the location of the grandest apartments, these edifices sought to pose as single-family Italian Renaissance palaces. A similar type is common in New York, reaching an apogee in McKim, Mead & White's 1911 apartment building at 998 Fifth Avenue.

Wagner's theories found concrete expression in two apartment buildings he designed on Vienna's Linke Wienzeile in 1898–99. The structures' façades have elaborate Jugendstil decoration, but their flat elevations, frameless windows, and use of new materials such as aluminum caused, in the words of an Austrian architectural critic, "a fuss." It is significant that the buildings failed to attract what Wagner saw as the new urban client, the man of business who was also a man of taste. Instead, in a scenario which would be repeated in New York, the apartments were rented by members of Vienna's bohemian world, writers, actors, and others connected with the nearby Theatre an der Wien.

Wagner's progress toward a cubistic modernism, a modernism which must be seen as a precursor of Art Deco, found full expression in one of his last projects, an apartment building on Neustiftgasse of 1912–13. Here exterior decoration is reduced to bands of black glass, while the edifice's minimal string course, its plain surface, and its set back uniform modular windows are design motifs which would become important elements in Art Deco architecture. Once again daring architecture drew almost exclusively creative clients, for at 40 Neustiftgasse among the renters were both Josef Hoffmann and Otto Wagner himself.

It is noteworthy that Otto Wagner's most distinguished disciple, Josef Hoffmann (1870–1956), should have found his most important patron for a domestic project not in Vienna, but in Brussels. This rapidly expanding capital of Belgium—newly rich from textiles, steel, and banking—was impressively receptive to new ideas in architecture and design. There in 1893, with his Villa Tassel, Victor Horta built what is arguably the first Art Nouveau residence in Europe. Hoffmann, collaborating with the painter Gustav Klimt and the designer Koloman Moser, created between 1906 and 1911 one of the germinal dwellings of the first half of the twentieth century, the Palais Stoclet. This enormous house, with its floral ornament confined into tight bands, its flat-roofed wing topped by a pergola constructed of square piers, its geometrical metalwork, and its tower whose crown is a series of receding sharp-edged masses, moves away from the curvilinear line of Art Nouveau into the geometry of Cubism, which is one of the foundations of Art Deco.

The Palais Stoclet is a pivotal connection between Viennese Secession and French Art Deco with its profound impact on American design. Once again a radical structure was made possible because of the artistic connections of the client. For though the Baron Adolphe Stoclet was a banker who had made a fortune in the Congo, his wife, Suzanne Stevens, was a member of a

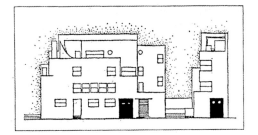 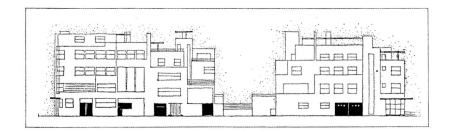

notable family of aesthetes. Among her relatives was Alfred Stevens (1823–1906), the fashionable portrait painter who counted among his patrons William Henry Vanderbilt and his son, William K., and Arthur Stevens, who discovered and promoted the work of Millet and Corot. The family had married into the equally impressive Mallets, one of whom, Maurice, a leading art appraiser, had been the first to recognize the importance of, among other painters, Sisley, Pissaro, Monet, Degas, and Manet. Maurice's son would become one of the preeminent Art Deco designers, and his uncle's Palais Stoclet was in a very real sense his architectural primer.

Born in Paris in 1886, Robert Mallet-Stevens was educated, not at the École des Beaux-Arts, but at the École Spéciale d'Architecture. Unlike the Beaux-Arts, which emphasized the meticulous rendering of the façades of buildings, the École Spéciale taught that the correct way to depict a building was by means of its volumes as though you were literally moving through its interior spaces. Mallet-Stevens early came under the influence of Auguste Perret (1874–1954), the father of modern French architecture and the teacher of Le Corbusier. Perret's apartment building on Paris's rue Benjamin-Franklin of 1902, one of the world's first structures to be constructed of reinforced concrete, presented a stripped-down geometric form that was unquestionably proto-Deco. As a young man Mallet-Stevens clearly delineated the architecture he felt the time summoned forth:

> Architectural problems and in particular the problems posed by stability, differ according to whether reinforced cement or weighty materials are used. Why then, in a new world, with new and powerful components available construct copies of old houses? The architecture presently being evolved will dispel these strange prejudices. Constructed in a rational way, tomorrow's home will be convenient, habitable, healthy, light, because that is how it ought to be. If it meets these requirements, it will achieve a type of beauty of its own.

As with Wagner and Hoffmann, Robert Mallet-Stevens's important residential commissions came from the elite worlds of fashion and the arts. One of the first, in 1913, was for a villa in the

Norman seaside resort of Deauville for Madame Paquin, who, along with Charles Frederick Worth, dominated French couture in the Belle Epoque. The outbreak of the First World War prevented her villa from being built, but in 1923, Mallet-Stevens was asked to design one of the most important dwellings constructed in France since the war. The location was the village of Hyères, perched on a high rocky cliff overlooking the Mediterranean. The clients were the Vicomte de Noailles, a famed amateur gardener, and his wife, Marie-Laure, a poet. Both were discerning and generous patrons of the arts. They wanted a totally new and original style of house and they got it. In this traditional Côte d'Azur village, which numbered among its inhabitants the American novelist Edith Wharton, Mallet-Stevens raised a striking and startlingly contemporary reinforced concrete villa whose horizontal façades of grey pebble dash, facing southward over the sea, fit perfectly into the rocky landscape. The de Noailles villa boasted a geometric garden, with a sculpture by Jacques Lipschitz, furniture by Pierre Chareau, bas-reliefs by Henri Laurens, and stained glass by Louis Barillet. It would be the setting for a famous surrealist film of 1928 by Man Ray, *Les Mystères du Château du Dé.*

In 1927 in Paris's fashionable 16th arrondissement, Mallet-Stevens completed an enclave of six villas for a group of avant-garde publishers, art dealers, sculptors, pianists, and filmmakers. One of the villas, the largest, he designed as his own residence and office. The dwellings lining both sides of the short cul-de-sac, which bears his name, present a related, rhythmical composition of cubistic volumes, cutout corner windows, metal ship-style railings, flat roofs, and dynamic square and round towers which instantly made them one of the icons of modern design. The street became a requisite stop for Americans, including Mrs. John D. Rockefeller, Jr., who were interested in contemporary art. As he was beginning to work on the rue Mallet-Stevens, the architect confidently proclaimed the triumphant advent of modern architecture and the end of provincialism: "The Normans are no more likely to return to the use of thatched roofs than to the donkey-drawn cart."

The Norman style, though, and numerous variations, such as Tudor and English half-timbered, was alive and well and living in New York. The stylistic tone had been set before the First World War when the Russell Sage Foundation had constructed Forest Hill Gardens on 142 acres in Queens. The landscape architect, Frederick Law Olmsted, Jr., and the architect, Grosvenor Atterbury, had designed a medieval village—complete with inn and church—in a picturesque Tudoresque style which would not have been out of place in some rural English county or even Normandy itself.

The reality was that, even in the most sophisticated precincts of Manhattan, the revolutionary, the iconoclastic aura surrounding Art Deco sharply restricted its use for residences, just as it had in Vienna and Paris. And there was another inhibiting factor, the feeling that Deco was slightly or even more than slightly risqué. This perception was the consequence of its being the style of choice in film for the abodes of those who were sinister or fast. This cinematic link between vice and modernity was born in 1924 when Mallet-Stevens designed a radically moderne

Art Deco poster for Marcel L'Herbier's 1923 film, *L'Inhumaine*. The poster is in the style of Fernand Léger, who designed one of the sets for the film. Other Art Deco designers who contributed to *L'Inhumaine* were Robert Mallet-Stevens (exterior design); Pierre Chareau (furniture), and René Lalique, Jean Puiforcat, and Jean Luce (decorative objects). (Private Collection.)

villa for the destructive, self-absorbed, pleasure-seeking singer, Claire Lescot—played by Georgette Leblanc—in Marcel L'Herbier's *L'Inhumaine*. Art Deco's suspect raffishness flashed on the American silver screen in 1928 with MGM's *Our Dancing Daughters*. Here art director Cedric Gibbons underscored the wild, sexy, liberated persona of the film's star, Joan Crawford, with sets whose geometric furniture, metal and frosted glass wall sconces, circular mirrors, and dramatically arched entranceways manifested the impact of the art director's visit to the 1925 Paris Exposition. Howard Mandelbaum and Eric Myers, in *Screen Deco,* succinctly sum up Hollywood's focused use of the style:

> If movies promised life, liberty, and the pursuit of riches, then Art Deco provided the perfect setting. Although characters were often permitted to live better than their incomes would normally allow, décor had to suit the situation. Obviously, films depicting the home life of a stuffy millionaire or struggling clerk could not present the latest in Deco design. Most closely associated with Art Deco were the nouveau riche, the underworld, the worlds of entertainment, travel, and retailing, and women either kept or liberated.

Thus it is not surprising that through the 1920s and into the 1930s almost all of the private townhouses constructed in Manhattan fit neatly into the architectural streetscape of Georgian, Adam, Italianate, and French styles which were the norm, particularly on the socially prestigious Upper East Side. Typical was the exquisite townhouse which, in 1930, Walker & Gillette designed for William Goadby Loew at 56 East 93rd Street. A suave limestone interpretation of 18th-century English precedents, it harmonized perfectly with a block where Florence Loew's father, George F. Baker, chairman of the board of the First National Bank, had built a majestic red brick Georgian mansion.

A notable deviation from the traditional New York townhouse was constructed by William Lescaze in 1934 at 211 East 48th Street. In the tradition of Mallet-Stevens, with his own house and office on the rue Mallet-Stevens, and the two villas Otto Wagner built for himself in Vienna,

A young Joan Crawford makes a flamboyant entrance in one of the stunning Art Deco sets of her 1928 film *Our Dancing Daughters*. The film was such a hit that MGM spun off two sequels, *Our Modern Maidens*, 1929, and *Our Blushing Brides*, 1930, both of which carried extravagant Art Deco design to the far corners of America. (Private Collection.)

ABOVE Walker & Gillette's William Goadby Loew house on East 93rd Street was an exemplary example of the traditional architecture favored by upper-class New Yorkers for their residences. (Contemporary Rendering by Chris Doyle. Private Collection.)

RIGHT The William Lescaze house and studio on East 48th Street was a radical reconstruction of a typical New York brownstone. (Historic Architecture Collection, The Art Institute of Chicago.)

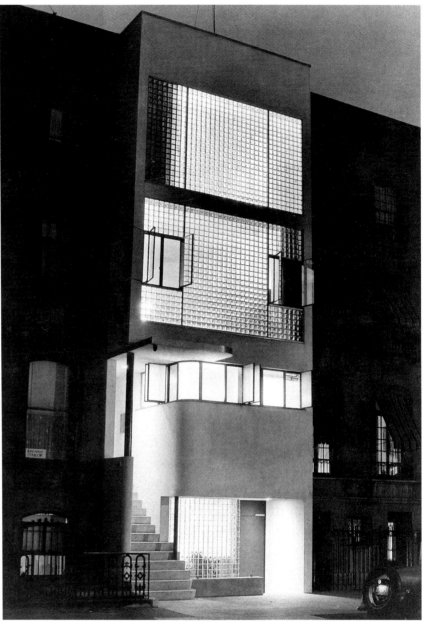

the East 48th Street structure encompassed a ground floor office for the architect, with, above that, his three-story apartment. The Swiss-born designer, who in 1930 had made a number of avant-garde proposals for a high-rise Museum of Modern Art and in 1931 had created a luxurious shop in tones of gold and gray with paneling of African walnut and other exotic woods for Hattie Carnegie, set down a truly revolutionary building near the romantic stucco Italianate houses of Turtle Bay Gardens. Though the Lescaze house has some International Style elements, its bold use of glass block and the elegant curve of its façade and band of windows at the second floor level give the structure an unmistakable Art Deco cast. This blending of the Deco and International styles is typical of the oeuvre of the eminent Parisian architect for whom Lescaze worked, Henri Sauvage. The revolutionary concomitant of the dwelling did not go unremarked. In an article on modern design in *Studio*, the critic Walter Rendell Storey wrote that William Lescaze occupied "a position with what might be described as the Left Wing of the movement."

A remarkable compromise between Art Deco and conventional taste was engineered at the high-stepped brownstone remodeled in 1928 at 132 East 71st Street by Drs. Ruth and Harry Bakwin. After the brownstone's façade and stoop were demolished and the structure pushed out to the pavement line, it was given a new unexceptional red brick pseudo-Georgian front. But behind that façade, the two physicians, both noted pediatricians, created a pair of remarkable Art Deco spaces. The library on the parlor floor, a high, almost square chamber, was lined in dark oak Art Deco paneling, given a teak floor, indirect cove lighting, and a modern-style fireplace whose mantel was topped by frosted glass which could be lit to display art objects. The room's furnishings, including a vast Deco library table, an upholstered sofa and two matching chairs, side chairs of richly burled walnut, and tables of macassar wood, were all purchased in Paris. They are very much in the manner of *D.I.M.*, the prestigious firm directed by René Joubert and Philippe Petit. On the fourth floor, in the Bakwins' office, everything was American-made, including black and gray Art Deco stepped bookcases, a Deco-style cornice, and cabinets with simple cubistic pewter pulls. The furniture, from the Empire Company, was also American.

Though the Bakwins, members of the upper reaches of New York society, would not appear to fit the typical profile of the Art Deco patron, a closer look reveals the artistic side behind the Georgian carapace. Both were important collectors of modern art, including the painters Cézanne, Modigliani, and Van Gogh and the sculptors Degas, Maillol, and Rodin. In addition, Ruth Bakwin was a sister of Nelson Morris, the Chicagoan who was the chief financier of the Parisian couturier Lucien Lelong, who employed Balmain, Dior, and Jacques Fath.

The same impulse which led progressive architects like Lescaze and avant-garde collectors like the Bakwins to be attracted to Art Deco also made it acceptable to institutions which felt that their mission would best be expressed by structures whose design was patently contemporary. Thus, when, in 1932, New York Hospital–Cornell Medical Center commissioned Coolidge, Shepley, Bulfinch & Abbott to design 11 buildings on a site between 68th and 70th streets and York Avenue and the East River, the architecture was not Palladian or Beaux Arts, though there

View across the East River of the New York Hospital–Cornell Medical Center by Coolidge, Shepley, Bulfinch & Abbott, completed in 1933. (Private Collection.)

were vestigial suggestions of the Gothic in the complex's ogee arched windows. Anchored by a 27-story tower, much the way Rockefeller Center is anchored by the RCA Building, the ensemble, in its dazzling white brick, its cubistic massing, and its touches of sunburst-like decoration, is one of New York's supreme Art Deco creations.

If a great teaching hospital wanted its structures to exemplify commitment to the latest in medical science, so too an educational institution founded in 1919 by scholars, like the radical economist Thorstein Veblen, historian Charles Beard, and education theorist John Dewey, did not want to evoke memories of the dreaming spires of Oxford. Faced in the late 1920s with the demolition of its original home on West 23rd Street to make way for the construction of the London Terrace apartments, the New School for Social Research engaged Joseph Urban to design a building for it on West 12th Street that would embody its progressive educational theories, such as the impor-

The New School's 550-seat auditorium's suspended perforated plaster ceiling makes it one of the city's best spaces acoustically. Its multiarched form was a precursor to the Radio City Music Hall. (Historic Architecture Collection, The Art Institute of Chicago.)

tance of classes for adults. While some architectural critics espied International Style elements in the edifice's striking seven-story façade, its boldly black-framed bands of windows, set between emphatically horizontal black-and-white brick spandrels which gave the building a wonderful sense of streamlined movement, clearly exemplified Viennese Secession melding into Art Deco. Additionally, in a very non–International Style gesture, the architect subtly recessed the façade as it rose, so that the New School's top floor is set a full foot further back than is the second. The purpose was to counter any sense at street level of brutal massiveness.

Certainly an institution such as the Museum of Modern Art, whose mission was, in the words of William S. Lieberman "to show the art of our time, of the moment," would not raise a structure which in any way suggested the European palaces inhabited by the Pierpont Morgan Library or the Frick Collection. The museum's agenda was essentially revolutionary. "Not many

With its bands of glass set in black frames and its black-and-white brick spandrels, Joseph Urban's New School for Social Research of 1930 on West 12th Street is one of New York's finest examples of the streamlined moderne style. (Historic Architecture Collection, The Art Institute of Chicago.)

One of the New School's great interior spaces which Urban paid particular attention to was the library on the fourth and fifth floors. The lounge, which he envisioned as a center of student social life, was above with a graceful double staircase leading down to the reading room. Urban's meticulous attention to detail is reflected in his choice of bronze for the handrails, not only because of the elegance of the material but also because of its pleasant tactile qualities. (Historic Architecture Collection, The Art Institute of Chicago.)

Americans liked modern art," Lieberman, the distinguished chairman emeritus of the Metropolitan Museum of Art's Modern Art Department, who began working at the Modern in the early 1940s, recalls.

> Of course there had been some exhibitions of modern art, notably the 1913 "Armory Show," and at Alfred Stieglitz's gallery, 291 Fifth Avenue, as well as at Katherine Dreier's "Société Anonyme," and at the Arts Club in Chicago, but these were rare. On the whole American taste was provincial. The Modern would exhibit cubism, surrealism, and abstract art. Its purpose was to counteract the cultural isolationism prevailing in the United States.

The Modern had been founded in 1929, primarily through the efforts of Abby Aldrich Rockefeller, wife of John D. Rockefeller, Jr.; the collector and patron Lizzie Bliss—the Museum's other trustees thought that "Lizzie" was not distingué and "Lizzie" became "Lillie"; and Mary Quinn Sullivan, an art dealer and close friend of both Mrs. Rockefeller and Miss Bliss. A west side location was originally considered, but it was quickly decided that the institution's mission of propagandizing for contemporary art could best be launched from midtown and the Modern opened on the 12th floor of the Heckscher Building at the southwest corner of Fifth Avenue and 57th Street. The first director was 27-year-old Alfred Barr, who had been recommended by Paul J. Sachs of Harvard's Fogg Museum.

With exhibitions of modern masters such as Paul Cézanne, Georges Seurat, Paul Gauguin, and Vincent van Gogh, attracting enormous crowds—much to the annoyance of the Heckscher's other tenants—the Museum was soon looking for a building of its own. In 1932, John D. Rockefeller, Jr., donated a townhouse at 11 West 53rd Street, which was the Museum's home until 1938. But the Modern, with its expanding new departments, such as those of architecture, film, and photography, desperately felt the need for more space. Eventually additional Rockefeller gifts of property on West 53rd Street provided a frontage of 130 feet, and fund-raising for an entirely new building began in earnest. In 1936 the commission was awarded to Philip L. Goodwin, a Museum trustee, and Edward Durrell Stone. Interestingly, Lieberman notes, continuing uncertainty about the Museum of Modern Art's future led to the building being designed in such a way that it could be used for other purposes. "While Goodwin and Stone were indeed the architects," Lieberman emphasizes, "the concept of the building was Alfred Barr's. He believed very firmly that a museum of modern art should be a place that one could encompass in a single visit. Alfred saw the museum's collection as not permanent. The older pictures would be eliminated, given or sold to museums such as the Metropolitan. Its collection would keep moving in time. It would not be an historical museum."

Modern art, particularly Cubist works by painters such as Picasso and Braque, could also be viewed in the Gallery of Living Art, later the Museum of Living Art, founded in 1927 by Albert Eugene Gallatin. Located in space provided by New York University in its Main Building on Washington Square East, the venue became associated in the 1930s with the American abstract painters Charles G. Shaw, George L. K. Morris, and Suzy Frelinghuysen, who because of their wealth and social position, along with Gallatin himself, became known as the "Park Avenue Cubists." The Museum of Living Art closed in 1942.

While the International Style, which had been championed by Barr and by the Museum, certainly occupied a niche in the architects' aesthetic consciousness, Goodwin's École des Beaux-Arts background and Stone's apprenticeship to Raymond Hood and Wallace K. Harrison at Rockefeller Center produced a façade with unmistakable French moderne flourishes. This is evident in the handsome dark blue tiles of the building's party walls, and in the huge window of Thermolux—a new translucent material substituted for the more expensive white Georgia marble the architects wanted—which bears little relationship to the galleries behind it. Just how far from the International Style the architects strayed is exemplified by the members' recessed terrace on the top floor whose canopy, punctuated with horizontal portholes, recalls the terrace atop Robert Mallet-Stevens's own house and studio in Paris and also the work of Frank Lloyd Wright, one of Edward Durrell Stone's heroes. A surprise and triumph of the Museum was its garden on the 54th Street side. "The garden was needed to exhibit contemporary sculpture which tended to be on a large scale, and was often designed to be seen out-of- doors," William Lieberman explains. "The garden was totally the creation of Alfred Barr."

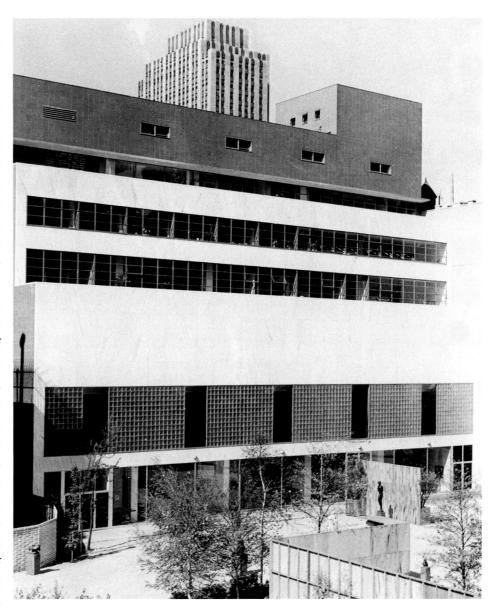

The garden of the Museum of Modern Art, 1939, was not only a perfect place to display large modern sculpture, but it was also a welcome oasis in the heart of the city. (Historic Architecture Collection, The Art Institute of Chicago.)

One of the most remarkable institutional appearances of Art Deco was in places of worship. Among the outstanding examples is the Salvation Army's combined Territorial Headquarters and Centennial Memorial Temple of 1930 on West 14th Street. For an organization with no attachment to past ecclesiastical styles, the architects, Voorhees, Gmelin & Walker, chose a bold Art Deco. The 11-story headquarters building is treated as a typical commercial high-rise struc-

ABOVE LEFT Detail of the entrance to the Salvation Army's Centennial Memorial Temple. (Photograph by John Cadenhead.)

ABOVE RIGHT An Art Deco rising sun, appropriate for an organization dedicated to bringing hope to the hopeless, is the dominant motif of the entrance gates to the Salvation Army Temple. (Photograph by John Cadenhead.)

ture, but there is nothing typical about the entrance to the 1,700-seat Temple. This vast triumphal arch, which focuses attention on the Army's battle cry, "Blood and Fire," inscribed on the Temple's wall, is one of the city's most powerful expressions of Deco.

Two Episcopal churches also embraced aspects of Art Deco as legatees of Bertram Grosvenor Goodhue, who, before his death in 1924, had forsaken Gothic for the Deco style embodied in his Nebraska State Capitol at Lincoln. Within Goodhue's awesome Byzantine-Romanesque nave of St. Bartholomew's Church on Park Avenue, Lee Lawrie, who had worked with the architect at Lincoln, created a dazzling golden Siena marble pulpit with, among other figures, a glorious Deco Moses and a cubistic angel wearing the full-bottomed wig of an English judge. Lawrie's lectern for St. Bartholomew's features a highly stylistic eagle, similar to those which perched

The Salvation Army Territorial Headquarters and Centennial Memorial Temple, 14th Street between Sixth and Seventh Avenues, is an Art Deco masterpiece by Voorhees, Gmelin & Walker. The name derives from the fact that the complex was begun in 1929, the hundredth anniversary of the birth of the Army's founder, William Booth. (The Salvation Army National Archives.)

atop moderne federal buildings across the country in the 1930s. Similarly, the Church of the Heavenly Rest on Fifth Avenue at 90th Street, completed in 1929 by Goodhue's successor firm, Mayers, Murray & Philip, also with sculpture by Lawrie, is of a stripped-down Gothic whose cubistic massing relates far more closely to Goodhue's Nebraska Capitol than to the Gothic Revival he had crafted with Ralph Adams Cram at St. Thomas Church on Fifth Avenue. Another brilliant exercise of early styles—here Romanesque and Gothic—transmogrifying into modernism is exemplified by McGill & Hamlin's Roman Catholic Church of the Most Precious Blood of 1932 in Astoria, Queens. Henry J. McGill, the partner in charge, gave the church a striking octagonal tower topped with aluminum pierced in a peacock pattern. Precious Blood's interior, a surprising Deco space enriched with terracotta, majolica, jewel-like art glass, and aluminum, is a tribute to the parish's and the architect's enthusiastic embrace of the most advanced trends in Catholic liturgical arts.

The geographic distribution of Deco-designed apartment buildings is sociologically revealing. Deco, on the whole, was not to the taste of Fifth and Park avenues. But it did appear between the two avenues in the distinguished 16-story limestone building designed in 1937 by Rosario Candela and Mott B. Schmidt at 19 East 72nd Street. While the overall form of the structure, with its side pavilions, is traditional, the decorative elements were flawless examples of Art Deco. Particularly notable are the beautifully rendered cyma moldings of the lower three floors which give the structure a stunning wavelike base, the moderne metal balcony railings, and the white marble entrance with charming symbols of nature and the arts by C. Paul Jennewein.

It is on Central Park West, a region that was ultima Thule for the Social Register, that the most spectacular specimens of Art Deco residential towers sprouted. Two of the finest are the Majestic at 115 Central Park West of 1930 and the Century apartments at 25 Central Park West of 1931. Both were the inspiration of the remarkable builder, Irwin C. Chanin, in collaboration with Jacques Delamarre and Sloan & Robertson. Chanin had originally planned a gargantuan hotel on the 115 Central Park West site, but after the Crash switched to an apartment house. The Majestic evokes a vis-

ABOVE Begun by Bertram Goodhue before the First World War, St. Bartholomew's Episcopal Church on Park Avenue between 50th and 51st streets was completed in 1927 by his successor firm of Mayers, Murray & Philip. St. Bartholomew's interior contains a number of significant examples of Deco religious art. Among them is the marble pulpit with its newel in the form of a very English recording angel by Lee Lawrie, the sculptor responsible for the *Atlas* at Rockefeller Center. (Private Collection.)

OPPOSITE A notable example of Gothic Revival melding into Art Deco is found at the Episcopal Church of the Heavenly Rest, southeast corner of Fifth Avenue and 90th Street, by Mayers, Murray & Philip. The upper elevations of the church's massive twin piers resemble the tops of skyscrapers. (Photograph by Samuel H. Gottscho. Courtesy Church of the Heavenly Rest.)

ceral verticality, a verticality underscored by its soaring ranks of windows set between powerful projecting piers which break through the roof lines of its two towers as though on their way to infinity. This insistent verticality is brilliantly countered on the structure's base by the horizontality of its broad corner windows, setting up a dynamic grid pattern reminiscent of a Piet Mondrian painting. In contrast, the Century's towers are crowded with compositions which evoke both the concepts of Italian Futurism and Art Deco's romance with the modern machine—turbos and dynamos. Viewed from Central Park they are among New York's most memorable images of 1930s modernism. It should be noted that a not inconsiderable number of those inhabiting the Majestic and the Century were writers, musicians, and actors.

Deco also flourished in the Bronx, where the magnificent apartment buildings of Horace Ginsbern made the Grand Concourse and Miami's South Beach almost mirror images. And it found niches outside Manhattan's more conventional neighborhoods. A stunning example is the Rockefeller Apartments at 17 West 54th Street of 1936, which Harrison & Fouilhoux designed to replace John D. Rockefeller, Sr.'s townhouse. Its turretlike rounded bays, with their encircling windows topped by parapets of glass, give the structure one of the city's most delightful façades. The façade also bears an uncanny resemblance to the luxury apartment building that Bassompierre, de Rutté and Sirvin completed in Paris at 7 rond-point du Pont-Mirabeau that same year.

Another classic example of Deco on the fringes are the Beaux-Arts Apartments created by Raymond Hood and Kenneth Murchison in 1931 at 307 and 310 East 44th Street. The twin edifices' emphatic linearity, their rough brick banding, and their sturdy metal industrial windows made them at once superb examples of Art Deco and good contextual neighbors to the buildings surrounding them. These were true studio loft buildings, having on their two upper floors double-height artist studios, with below, small studio apartments—also double height—equipped with Murphy beds. Since most of the flats possessed only a small serving pantry, room service was provided by a restaurant on the ground floor—the Café Bonaparte—decorated by Winold Reiss.

Appropriately, the Beaux-Arts Apartments became one of the centers in the city for the French artists who had fled Paris in the wake of the German occupation. Donald Gurney, who himself had been an American expatriate in Paris and who resided at the Beaux-Arts during the Second World War, recalled those extraordinary times: "I would often give cocktail parties to see old friends and typically André Breton, Yves Tanguy, Antoine de Saint-Exupéry, Marcel Duchamp, and others, would come. Being friends, everyone talked and smoked. I had inherited a canary from the previous tenant and one morning, after such a party, I found the poor thing dead in its cage. The cigarette smoke had been too much for it."

Though the Deco note might be struck by the exteriors of the apartment buildings in which they lived, it took a bit of audacity for New Yorkers to carry the style inside. An instructive example is the 17-story apartment building which Rosario Candela and Arthur Loomis Harmon designed at the northwest corner of Park Avenue and 71st Street in 1930–31. Its exterior has some

Nineteen East 72nd Street at the northwest corner of Madison Avenue by Candela and Schmidt replaced the vast Richardsonian mansion Stanford White designed for jeweler Charles Tiffany in 1882. (The Wurts Collection, Museum of the City of New York.)

The Majestic Apartments of 1930, southwest corner of Central Park West and 72nd Street, were one of New York's many notable Deco structures which owed their inception to developer Irwin S. Chanin. The building's decorative elements were the work of sculptor René Chambellan. (The Wurts Collection, Museum of the City of New York.)

TOP These decorative elements by Horace Ginsbern reveal the architect's profound debt to the design vocabulary of the 1925 Paris Exposition. Indeed the structures built on the Grand Concourse in the 1930s, its golden age, comprise one of the city's most impressive Art Deco enclaves. (Avery Architectural and Fine Arts Library, Columbia University.)

BOTTOM Ginsbern's Town Towers Apartments of 1931, on the Bronx's Grand Concourse at 197th Street, are one of the many splendid Art Deco buildings on this thoroughfare. The completion of the Independent subway in 1933 linked the Concourse to Midtown Manhattan and to the Garment District where many of its residents were employed. (Avery Architectural and Fine Arts Library, Columbia University.)

OPPOSITE The distinctive glass bays of the Rockefeller Apartments were originally intended to provide space for "dinettes," a very 1930s concept. The twin buildings at 17 West 54th Street and 24 West 55th Street occupied the site of John D. Rockefeller, Sr.'s townhouse. ( Historic Architecture Collection. The Art Institute of Chicago.)

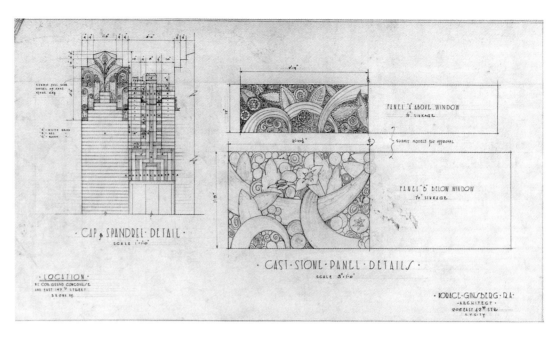

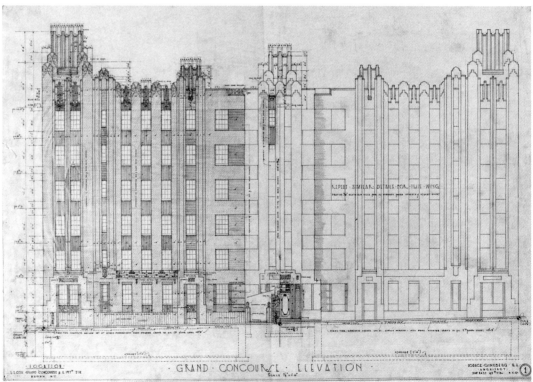

Located in a rather dingy neighborhood of tenements and commercial structures on East 44th Street between First and Second Avenues, the Beaux-Arts Apartments had originally been conceived in the late 1920s as a way to provide space for architects and artists. The incentive came from the presence of the Beaux-Arts Institute of Design, which had moved to 304 East 44th Street in 1928. The Institute followed closely in its art and architecture courses the academic tradition of Paris's École des Beaux-Arts. (Photograph by John Cadenhead.)

handsome, if timid, Art Deco elements, particularly the tall columns topped by florally festooned moderne urns flanking the Park Avenue entrance. The sleek striated gray marble outer lobby, the marble laid in severe geometric patterns, resembles nothing so much as the entrance to the vault of a very solvent Wall Street bank. But the tenants of its vast duplexes—including the John D. Rockefeller, Jr.'s in their 24-room spread—almost universally opted for Sheraton over Chareau, Louis over Lalique. But in an astounding *volte-face*, Nelson Rockefeller at 810 Fifth Avenue, a typical limestone Beaux Arts–style building, commissioned the prominent Paris decorator Jean Michel Frank (1895–1941) to design interiors for his apartment. The project was completed in 1938. In the brightly colored living room, Frank composed a brilliant design vignette by placing a pale yellow sofa of his own design and a red coffee table beneath a great 1931 Picasso still life rich in greens and yellows.

Yet the city did have designers eager to break with the tradition of chintz, Chinoiserie, and Chippendale promoted by Elsie de Wolfe and other popular interior decorators and follow the path toward modernity blazed at the 1925 Paris Exposition by Émile-Jacques Ruhlmann and others. And the furniture of the leading French designers was readily available in the city's department stores. Among the leaders of those embracing the new style was Paul T. Frankl, who arrived in New York from Vienna in 1914 and whose Frankl Galleries were one of New York's most influential design centers. Other stars in the new firmament were Gilbert Rohde, who would be a significant advocate for Art Deco at the 1939 World's Fair, and Lee Simonson, originally a theater set designer, who, in the late 1920s, became a major champion of the new taste. In 1939 the *Studio* singled out Simonson as one of the nation's leading modernists: "Some designers like Lee Simonson predict that the home of the future will be largely furnished when the house is built. In a suite furnished by Mr. Simonson in an apartment hotel, a couch was combined with book shelves and cupboards, while a radio cabinet, as well as a desk and console tables as permanent fixtures, insured both that less furniture needed to be installed and that the decorative balance, as planned by the designer, would be retained."

Undoubtedly, though, the most influential Deco designer was Donald Deskey. Born in Minnesota in 1894 and educated at the

This room by the superb French *ébéniste* Émile-Jacques Ruhlmann was the type which had a profound effect on progressive New York designers. A star of the 1925 Paris Exposition, Ruhlmann was greatly admired by Americans, such as Ely Jacques Kahn. (Roger-Viollet.)

In this 1930s interior, designer Gilbert Rohde focused on two important elements of Art Deco interior decoration, the curved wall and the horizontal subdivision of walls by the use of matte and shiny metallic finishes. (Private Collection.)

University of California's School of Architecture and at the Art Institute of Chicago and in Paris, he arrived in New York early in the 1920s. Beginning as an industrial designer, Deskey soon switched to creating brilliantly innovative residential interiors. In 1929 he caused a sensation with his Fifth Avenue apartment for Adam Gimbel, president of Saks Fifth Avenue, which sported cork walls and copper ceilings. Deskey's most daunting commission came in 1934, when the 4-foot, 10-inch cosmetics queen, Helena Rubinstein, asked him to bring modernity to her 895 Park Avenue apartment. Amidst the dwelling's pack-rat-like collection of School of Paris paintings, Empire furniture, and African art, Deskey introduced a touch of rational design by coloring the walls white and, wherever possible, covering surfaces with the material of the moment, cellophane.

That special confluence of personality and taste which led patrons to choose Art Deco for their residences is perfectly exemplified by Katherine Brush and her husband, Charles Hubert Winans.

The living room of the apartment at 322 East 57th Street that Joseph Urban designed in the early 1930s for Katherine Brush and Charles Hubert Winans was a *soigné* composition of black and white. The enormous L-shaped sofa was covered in white leather. (Private Collection.)

ABOVE RIGHT In 1934 the Metropolitan Museum of Art staged its second Exhibition of Contemporary American Industrial Art. The first, in 1929, had featured luxurious rooms and furnishings by, among others, Joseph Urban, Raymond Hood, and Ely Jacques Kahn. The new exhibition, launched during the austere 1930s, attempted to display furniture and objects within the reach of everyman. It drew some 130,000 visitors. Among the rooms in the 1934 show was this dining room by Donald Deskey featuring a glass block wall. (Historic Architecture Collection, The Art Institute of Chicago.)

ABOVE LEFT An office designed by Lee Simonson and Raymond Loewy for the 1934 Metropolitan Museum exhibit. (Historic Architecture Collection, The Art Institute of Chicago.)

Both were highly sophisticated individuals and both were involved in the arts, he as an important patron of Paul Frankl and she as a popular author of worldly novels, including *Red-Headed Woman* and *Young Man of Manhattan*. Katherine Brush was a habitué of El Morocco. Lucius Beebe, who chronicled the foibles of Elmo's regulars, said that she had a different colored typewriter for every day of the week. The apartment at 322 East 57th Street was truly historic, for it was the only domestic interior designed by Joseph Urban and, in addition, was his last work, completed in 1933, the year of his death. The two-story living room was meticulously crafted by Urban as a background for glamorous entertaining. Its walls were vividly colored red and black and white and its geometric fireplace was topped by a circular mirror 10 feet in diameter which reflected its twin across the room. The enormous L-shaped white leather sofa, the pair of banquettes placed within niches, and the luxurious Deco club chairs intentionally gave the chamber the atmosphere, not of a home, but of a nightclub. The effect was heightened by the metal ship's railings of the balcony leading to the apartment's dining room, which made this, in 1930's parlance, a "studio." The Brush apartment, wherein the tick-tock of the old-fashioned grandfather's clock has been replaced by the rattle of ice cubes in a silver martini shaker, would have been a perfect set for Cole Porter's sublime 1934 musical, *Anything Goes*:

> *In olden days, a glimpse of stocking*
> *Was looked on as something shocking.*
> *But now, God knows,*
> *Anything goes.*
> *Good authors too who once knew better words*
> *Now only use four-letter words,*
> *Writing prose,*
> *Anything goes.*
> *If driving fast cars you like*
> *If low bars you like,*
> *If old hymns you like,*
> *If bare limbs you like*
> *If Mae West you like*
> *Or me undressed you like,*
> *Why, nobody will oppose.*
> *When ev'ry night, the set that's smart is intruding*
> *   in nudist parties in*
> *Studios,*
> *Anything goes.*

Straw marquetry table by Jean Michel Frank, who designed rooms for the Nelson Rockefellers, ca.1932. Frank's view of interior decoration was architectural, and his furniture is often a stylish combination of restrained geometric design with sumptuous veneers such as vellum, sharkskin, suede, and straw marquetry. (Courtesy Maison Gerard, Ltd.)

   This is, of course, exactly what those who chose Art Deco hoped to evoke—up-to-the-minute Gothamite sophistication; and this is also, of course, what those who chose Chippendale feared that the style represented. Mrs. Post had not been wrong when she warned about "revolution" emanating from Paris.

# THE ROCKEFELLERS' CENTER

Great cities have places that encapsulate their very essence. One thinks immediately of London's Trafalgar Square, Paris's place de la Concorde, and Venice's Piazza San Marco. In New York the true heart of the metropolis is undoubtedly Rockefeller Center.

The 1939 *WPA Guide to New York City* puts it concisely: "In its architecture Rockefeller Center stands as distinctly for New York as the Louvre stands for Paris." Turning in from Fifth Avenue to the Channel Gardens, one moves away from the roar of traffic and enters something very rare in American cities, a precinct of planned space, with sunlight and flowers and the splash of water. In its subtle combination of luxury and business, of commerce and the arts, Rockefeller Center achieves—subtly but inescapably—a peerless urbanity. Ironically when, on March 5, 1931, a tentative model for the project was unveiled, it was greeted by almost universal hisses. "Radio City is ugly. Its exterior is revoltingly dull and dreary," the New York *Herald Tribune* proclaimed. The *New York Times* was equally dismissive, calling the maquette a composition of "architectural aberrations."

It was something of a miracle that 12 acres of underdeveloped property with a single ownership existed in midtown Manhattan in the 20th century. The tale behind this phenomenon stretches back to the infancy of the nation. Doctor David Hosack, a native New Yorker, combined brilliance and irresistible charm with a fine medical education received in America and the British Isles. Hosack, a firm believer in the curative power of plants, was a professor at Columbia College of both botany and materia medica, the study of the composition of medical remedies. His dream was to establish a botanical garden in New York which would rival the great ones of Europe, such as the Jardin des Plantes in Paris and the Chelsea Physic Garden in London. When his efforts to have either Columbia or the State of New York underwrite his project came to naught, Hosack decided to take on the task himself. His efforts to find a suitable site led him to 20 acres lying between the Middle Road (now Fifth Avenue) on the east and the Albany Road (now Sixth Avenue) to the west, which were part of the common lands. Because the tract was rock-strewn and lay some three miles north of the built-up part of Manhattan Island, the city fathers were glad to be rid of it. In 1801 Dr. Hosack agreed to pay $4,807.36 in cash, plus a quitrent of 16 bushels of wheat a year.

Hosack christened his demesne "The Elgin Botanical Garden," after his father's native town in Scotland, and set about turning the tract into one of the wonders of New York. But the good doctor, characterized by a fellow physician as "a man of profuse expenditure," had soon spent more than $100,000, an astonishing sum. When his expectations that his costs would be offset by the sale of medicinal plants and the products of his nursery failed to materialize, he turned again for help to Columbia and the state. But once more he was turned down and, in 1810, the

OPPOSITE  The RKO Roxy at the southeast corner of Sixth Avenue and 49th Street was the first Rockefeller Center Building to be completed. It was named for Samuel Lionel Rothafel, aka "Roxy," an impresario famed for his crowd-pleasing presentations which included both films and vaudeville acts. Constructed specifically to exhibit sound motion pictures, the theater was designed by the firms of Hood & Fouilhoux; Reinhard & Hofmeister; and Corbett, Harrison & MacMurray who worked at Rockefeller Center under the collective name Associated Architects. Its restrained Art Deco exterior was a sharp contrast to Rothafel's Spanish Revival Roxy of 1927 on West 51st Street. The interiors, by Eugene Schoen, continued the note of restrained Deco modernism. The RKO Roxy opened in December 1932, the same month as the Radio City Music Hall. But the threat of a lawsuit by the owners of the old Roxy quickly forced the Rockefeller management to change its name to the colorless Center Theater. From the beginning, the 3,500-seat theater had difficulty competing with the nearby, far more glamorous Music Hall. The Center Theater was demolished in 1954. (Private Collection.)

very year that he had made his final payment on the property, Hosack ended up selling it to the State of New York for $75,000.

The subsequent linkage to Columbia, which was to keep the site together, had little to do with Dr. Hosack. The college, located on what it called its "Lower Estate" on Park Place between Church Street and Broadway, had long sought financial aid from the state. But while other educational and even religious institutions had received help, Columbia had been regularly rebuffed—because, some said, of its close association before the Revolution with the overwhelmingly Loyalist Anglican Church. (Founded as King's College in 1754, the institution closed during the Revolution. When the college reopened in 1784, it adopted the less monarchical name of Columbia.) In 1814 the State of New York organized a lottery to help Union and Hamilton colleges, and once again turned down Columbia when it asked for a share of the proceeds. But the legislature, seeing a way to dispose of Dr. Hosack's botanical garden while offering at least something to Columbia, presented the tract to the college. The trustees, who had been seeking money to finance a move from the cramped quarters that had housed the college since its founding, felt that once more they had been short-changed. Until 1828 they were apparently correct. In that year, though, Columbia found a long-term tenant for the property who would pay cash. By the 1850s, when the college decided to move uptown, the property, now assessed at $550,000, had grown too valuable for it to build on. Instead, Columbia bought the New York Institution for the Deaf and Dumb's building on Madison Avenue between 49th and 50th streets and settled there in 1857. To help pay for the move, it sold 16 lots of what it called its "Upper Estate" and divided the remainder of the property into 272 lots and rented them under 21-year leases, renewable for an additional 21 years. Columbia had the right to purchase the buildings if either the college or the tenant failed to renew. Four decades later, to finance its 1897 migration to a new Morningside Heights campus, Columbia sold one block of its Upper Estate, reducing the tract to just under 13 acres. During the real estate boom which engulfed Manhattan in the 1870s, Columbia's Upper Estate flourished. Along Fifth Avenue, four- and five-story stone-fronted houses sprang up, while in the cross streets behind them rose uniform rows of modest brownstones. By the beginning of the 20th century, most of the Fifth Avenue residences had been converted into shops and offices, and while the brownstones close to Fifth Avenue continued to be desirable, those to the west, near the clamor of the Sixth Avenue elevated, had declined into rooming houses. By the 1920s much of the college's property had degenerated into a notorious district of speakeasies and brothels.

Yet this black cloud had a silver lining. Most of the leases on the property were due to run out between 1928 and the end of the decade. With the stock market reaching new highs every day and New York in the midst of an unprecedented building boom, Columbia envisioned a bonanza from the redevelopment of its property. At the center of these plans was the Metropolitan Opera, housed since 1883 in what wags snidely labeled "the yellow brewery," an ugly brick structure occupying the block bounded by Broadway, Seventh Avenue, and 39th and 40th streets. Prodded by its most powerful board member, Otto Kahn, a partner in the prestigious Kuhn, Loeb & Co. investment banking firm, the opera was actively considering constructing a more glamorous house in a more fashionable neighborhood. In January 1926 Kahn presented the opera's board of directors with a memorandum that outlined a plan to finance the move. With the Coolidge boom reaching stratospheric heights, Kahn estimated that the opera could sell its old property for $12 million and that a new house would cost $8.5 million to build, leaving $3.5 million for the purchase of a site.

John Tonnele, a vice president of the highly respected real estate firm of William A. White & Company, got wind of the decision to move to a more elegant quarter. His company was Columbia's advisor on the development of its Upper Estate, and an opera house immediately struck him as the ideal magnet to attract upscale tenants to the property. Benjamin Wistar Morris, the architect engaged by the opera board to draw up plans for the new house, was excited by the possibilities of the spacious site. Morris, whose other projects at the time included a superb addition to the Pierpont Morgan Library, sketched a grand opera house in the Art Deco style fronting a broad plaza. Surrounding the opera house, the architect envisioned seven other buildings—hotels, apartment houses, and department stores—all linked by a promenade and set amid gardens and fountains. The prototype of what was to become Rockefeller Center had been born. The only missing component now was a Rockefeller, and that key piece of the puzzle was about to be added.

In order to spur interest in the project, on May 21, 1928, Kahn and the other Metropolitan Opera directors hosted a dinner at the palatial Metropolitan Club on Fifth Avenue. They invited some of the city's richest men, including John D. Rockefeller, Jr., son of the founder of the Standard Oil Company. He was not able to attend, but Ivy Lee, the public relations genius who worked for him, did. Four days after the dinner, Lee sent Rockefeller a memo noting that, with the opera house as its focal point, the Upper Estate site could become "the most valuable shopping district in the world." Intrigued, Rockefeller initially expressed interest merely in joining a large syndicate which would take over the leases of the Upper Estate for 99 years. When the idea of such a syndicate failed to attract backers, he began thinking of taking on the entire project alone. John D. Rockefeller, Jr., quickly opened his own negotiations with Columbia and by the summer of 1928 reached an agreement giving him the right to buy part of the Upper Estate for $6 million and to lease the rest for 21 years at $3.3 million a year. An appraisal valued the property at $62 million.

The Rockefellers had always been in the habit of seeking the best advice on any subject and, more remarkably, heeding it. Now John D. Rockefeller, Jr., turned to John R. Todd, the attorney who headed the Todd & Brown engineering firm. He was a man who understood the complexi-

John D. Rockefeller, Sr., and John D. Rockefeller, Jr., about 1915. (Private Collection.)

Bird's-eye view of Rockefeller Center in a rendering by John Wenrich. The pedestrian bridges across 49th and 50th streets were never built. (© 2004 Rockefeller Group International, Inc.)

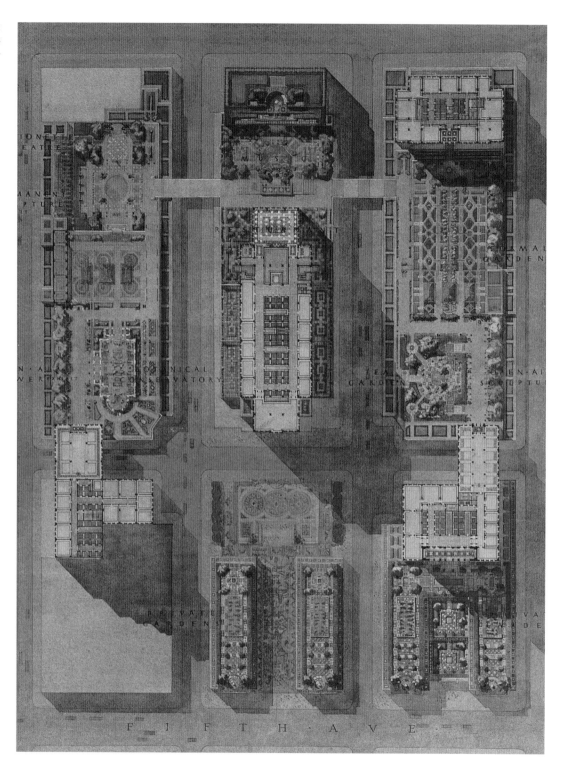

ties of urban construction and of matching the right client to a property as few men did. It was Todd who now brought in L. Andrew Reinhard and Henry Hofmeister, the first architects of the team that would eventually create Rockefeller Center. Both were in their late thirties. Hofmeister specialized in ventilation, plumbing, and the arrangement of interiors, while Reinhard was both a designer and a top-notch drafts-man. Working over the summer, by September 1928 they had produced proposals that became known in the history of Rockefeller Center as "The Labor Day Plans." The mix of structures included office towers, a 37-story hotel, and a 35-story apartment building.

That autumn, lawyers crafted the formal agreement, and on January 22, 1929, the president of Columbia University, Nicholas Murray Butler, publicly announced the details. The *New York Times* reported that the ensemble, with its open plaza, exclusive shops, and cafés, was reminiscent of Paris's place de l'Opéra. Now that the agreement was approved, the pace of the project picked up. Rockefeller, with the advice of the eminent architects John Russell Pope and William T. Aldrich, invited several other leading architects to submit designs by May 1929, designs that all who signed subleases would have to follow in their buildings. Two of the architects chosen, Raymond M. Hood and Wallace K. Harrison, would have a singular influence in shaping Rockefeller Center. Hood, a Rhode Islander educated at Brown University, was the center's supreme aesthetician. Like such seminal American architects as Richard Morris Hunt, Louis Sullivan, and Charles F. McKim, Hood had studied architecture at the École des Beaux-Arts in Paris. Then—and significantly—he had worked in the office of America's leading practitioners of the Gothic Revival style, Cram, Goodhue & Ferguson. In 1922, he and his partner, John Mead Howells, had won the competition to design the new *Chicago Tribune* headquarters, beating out Eliel Saarinen's avant-garde entry with a 36-story Gothic-style skyscraper. Raymond Hood's mastery of Gothic design strongly appealed to

John Wenrich's 1935 rendering of Rockefeller Center. (© 2004 Rockefeller Group International, Inc.)

Rockefeller. That style was the family's first choice for public commissions: one of the supreme examples of Gothic Revival in the Midwest, their Rockefeller Memorial Chapel at the University of Chicago by Bertram Grosvenor Goodhue, had just been completed, and now John D. Rockefeller, Jr., was deeply involved in the construction of Allen & Collens's and Henry C. Pelton's splendid French Gothic–inspired Riverside Church, the family's future place of worship. Rockefeller's vision was of a complex sheathed in a Gothic style which would meld perfectly with James Renwick's St. Patrick's Cathedral across Fifth Avenue.

Wallace Harrison, a 35-year-old from Massachusetts, had also studied at the École des Beaux-Arts. He had been a draftsman in the firm of McKim, Mead & White and was currently the junior partner of the noted architect Harvey Wiley Corbett. Harrison had two advantages over the other architects working on the project: he had been a draftsman for Raymond Hood and thus was close to the master architect of the center, and he was married to the sister-in-law of John D. Rockefeller, Jr.'s only daughter, Abby.

During the summer of 1929 the architects, lawyers for the Metropolitan Opera, and Rockefeller's advisors held numerous meetings, some at the Rockefeller summer home at Seal Harbor, Maine, to discuss architectural details and plans. By October the preliminary drawings for the project had been finished. Benjamin Wistar Morris was the architect of the opera house, and the other architects—Reinhard, Hofmeister, Corbett, Harrison, and Hood—had charge of the surrounding structures. The magnitude of the undertaking now began to fully dawn upon the participants. With its 14 major buildings, this was the largest private development the world had ever seen.

Everything, though, was about to change. On October 29, 1929, the stock market crashed. In the wake of the millions lost that day, the plans for the Upper Estate would be completely transformed. The first casualty was the opera. With its property plunging in value and Otto Kahn's health failing, there was no chance that it could raise the funds for a new house. What the opera left behind for the planners was both the vision of focusing the project on a central imposing edifice and the concept of an open plaza. Rockefeller was determined to proceed. He had little choice. As he observed afterward: "The general financial situation was so steadily getting worse that there was no possibility of subletting unimproved, as contemplated, any portion of the area. There were only two courses open to me. One, to abandon the entire development. The other, to go forward with it in the definite knowledge that I myself would have to build and finance it alone." Suddenly, instead of being driven by the need for a hall for *Rigoletto* and *Tannhäuser*, the enterprise would become unabashedly a business venture, a monument to commerce.

In 1930, bulldozers began clearing the site upon which would rise the structures designed by a team of 30 architects and 120 draftsmen working in the Graybar Building on Lexington Avenue next to Grand Central Terminal. The troublesome question of what would replace the opera house as the focus of the complex had not been answered. The solution would come from an unexpected source. That it came at all was mere good luck. Raymond Hood had been remodeling space on Fifth Avenue for new studios and offices for NBC, where David Sarnoff was pioneering the idea that radio could not only provide entertainment for the entire family but be an important advertising medium as well. Sarnoff wanted to construct large sound-proof auditoriums and recording studios with dust-free control panels. The Rockefeller project seemed a perfect fit for NBC's parent company, the Radio Corporation of America. With its two New York stations, WEAF and WJZ, its two networks, the Red and the Blue, and its Radio-Keith-Orpheum (RKO) movie and theater operations, RCA was desperate, not only for the broadcasting facilities Sarnoff wanted, but for prime office space and two theaters. For that, RCA was willing to pay more than $4.25 million a year in rent. In the spring of 1930 the new focus of the project became the RCA Building. Curiously, the Metropolitan Opera did in a way come to Rockefeller Center. It would be NBC, every Saturday afternoon in the season, with Milton Cross explaining the music and plots during intermission, which broadcast live opera from the stage of the Metropolitan.

The structure presented Raymond Hood with the opportunity to create one of the masterpieces of 1930s Art Deco urban design. By 1930 the architect had

The 70-story RCA Building under construction. (Bibliothèque Historique de la Ville de Paris.)

shed his Gothic garb for the sleek raiment of the Deco style. That very year he had proved his mastery of it in his stunning Daily News Building on East 42nd Street. It wasn't only Hood's enthusiasm for the streamlined modernity of Art Deco that overcame Rockefeller's initial yearning after Gothic. Rockefeller's wife, Abby Aldrich, and his son, Nelson, were both avid and

RIGHT The lobby of the RCA building showing the new high-speed elevators which could whisk passengers upward at 1,400 feet per minute. (Historic Architecture Collection, The Art Institute of Chicago.)

OPPOSITE Details of Lee Lawrie's sculpture *Wisdom with Light and Sound* above the main entrance to the RCA Building (now the General Electric Building). The left arm and hand of Wisdom, carved in limestone, points downward to the multifaceted glass screen (240 pieces, made by Corning) below, symbolizing light and sound. (Photographs by John Cadenhead.)

The Fifth Avenue entrance to the British Empire Building by Associated Architects. The entrance is crowned by the arms of the British monarch. Below it is Paul Jennewein's gilded bronze relief illustrating *Industries of the British Commonwealth*, with, among other figures, that of a fisherman, coal miner, and shepherd. (Photograph by Esther Bubley, Standard Oil Company of New Jersey Collection, Eckstrom Library, University of Louisville.)

knowledgeable collectors of contemporary sculpture and painting. They both came down on the modernist side with all the force family members can bring to bear. In addition, engineer Todd recognized the key economic reality in constructing contemporary buildings. Speaking of the type of architects he sought for the project, Todd commented, "We didn't want men who were too much committed to the architectural past or who were too much interested in wild modernism." What the center desired was "good plans for what we had to have and then to clothe those plans, as simply and attractively as possible, with clean-looking exteriors."

Art Deco fitted these specifications perfectly and the style had one further advantage. It was, above all else, an optimistic architecture, one inspired by the belief that out of the modern laboratory and the factory would come a better world, an architecture that radiated an incontestable belief in progress. And progress would become the theme of every aspect of Rockefeller Center. Hood's 70-story limestone-clad RCA Building, with its rhythmic setbacks expressing both the Cubism beloved by Art Deco as well as the declension of its elevator banks, is a hymn to modernity, to a sunny future, to all the scientific wonders that the 20th century encompassed. It manifests power and light and energy.

But the ground the edifice rose upon was not yet, officially, Rockefeller Center. It was no easy task to persuade the diffident John D. Rockefeller, Jr., to permit the family name to be used in connection with the development, especially since muckrakers and others had pilloried the family for decades as unrepentant "robber barons." But once the opera had withdrawn from the project, the designation of "Metropolitan Square" seemed to be both insipid and misleading. At the same time, "Radio City" was beginning to be applied not only to the RCA Building but to the entire venture. With other corporations who had signed subleases unhappy at the prospect of having another corporation's name as their address, the complex's management insisted that a new appellation be found. John Todd pushed for "Rockefeller," but, as Nelson Rockefeller later recalled, his father agreed only after he was persuaded that "this would be a sound thing and a creditable institution." On April 17, 1932,

Columbia's Upper Estate finally became Rockefeller Center. It was right that it should be so, for it was because of John D. Rockefeller, Jr., that the complex was "sound" and "creditable." It was only because he had consented to be personally responsible for repayment that the Metropolitan Life Insurance Company agreed to lend the enterprise $65 million at 5 percent. It was Rockefeller who, in the darkest days of the Depression, kept things going by selling Standard Oil of New York stock, which had been valued at $80 a share a decade earlier, for $2 a share to pay construction expenses. Most significantly, it was Rockefeller who insisted on "the last 5 percent," that is, spending one-twentieth extra to get top quality. Good taste and finesse inform Rockefeller Center's every aspect, beginning with the buildings' cladding of fine gray Indiana limestone sawed by a special process to texture it, rather than brick as originally suggested.

The first chance for the public to truly see the last 5 percent in Rockefeller Center came on December 27, 1932, when Radio City Music Hall opened its doors. Passing through the restrained black marble ticket lobby, visitors entered the 60-foot-high grand foyer, aglow with 29-foot-long crystal chandeliers, tall bronzed glass mirrors, and Ezra Winter's vast mural *The Fountain of Youth*. This was but a prelude to one of the world's most awesome Deco interiors, the stupendous 6,200-seat auditorium, whose ceiling, consisting of 180-degree arcs of light curving down to the floor, was inspired, the music hall's impresario, Samuel "Roxy" Rothafel, announced, by a sunset he had viewed from the stern of an ocean liner. For the opening night audience, Roxy staged a mind-numbing six-hour variety show.

The presence of the work of artists such as Ezra Winter at the music hall was not a matter of chance. In 1932, Rockefeller set aside $150,000 for artworks to enhance the center and formed an Advisory Art Commission to find painters and sculptors to make the project "as beautiful as possible." The Rockefeller impulse was at one with the enthusiastic embrace by Art Deco architects of painting, sculpture, and mosaic, as well as other art forms, to enhance their structures.

Howells & Hood's Daily News Building, 220 East 42nd Street, was begun in 1929 and completed in 1931. The vertical white structure, a brilliant interplay of cubistic volumes, was the conception of Raymond Hood. It was a revolutionary departure from Howells & Hood's Gothic Chicago Tribune Tower completed in 1925. (Private Collection.)

Hood imbued the Art Deco black glass lobby rotunda of the Daily News Building with a sense of drama by placing at its center a revolving globe lit from below. He would bring that sense of architectual drama to Rockefeller Center. (Avery Architectural and Fine Arts Library, Columbia University.)

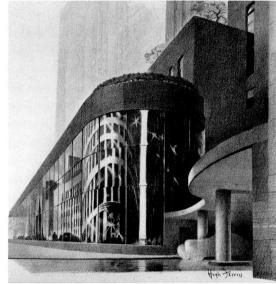

ABOVE Hugh Ferriss's rendering of the Eastern Airlines Building, 10 Rockefeller Plaza. This building by Associated Architects was the next-to-last structure completed in the original Rockefeller Center plan. (Avery Architectural and Fine Arts Library, Columbia University.)

LEFT Isamu Noguchi's stainless-steel bas-relief on the theme of news gathering proclaims the purpose of the Associated Press Building. (Photograph by John Cadenhead.)

The galaxy of artists contributing to the splendor of Rockefeller Center is truly remarkable. Among them is René Chambellan, who sculpted the bronze fountains consisting of Tritons and Nereids for the Channel Gardens; Paul Manship, creator of *Prometheus,* which presides over the sunken central plaza; José María Sert, the Spanish painter, responsible for the imposing mural on the west wall of the RCA Building's main lobby; Gaston Lachaise, the designer of the four panels symbolizing various aspects of modern civilization on the Sixth Avenue façade of the RCA Building; Hildreth Meiere, who crafted the 18-foot-diameter metal plaques representing the theater for the southern elevation of Radio City Music Hall; Stuart Davis, whose witty painting brightened the Music Hall's men's smoking lounge; and Isamu Noguchi, the sculptor of the stainless steel celebration of the business of news gathering which sits above the entrance to the Associated Press Building.

ABOVE  Stuart Davis's 12-by 18-foot painting in the men's smoking lounge had for its theme "Men Without Women" which humorously depicted the pastimes males turn to when they are deprived of female companionship, among them horse racing, sailing, and, naturally, pipe smoking. (Photograph by Thurman Rotan, 1933, Canadian Centre for Architecture, Montreal.)

OPPOSITE  The determination of Donald Deskey, who was in charge of decorating all of the Music Hall's interiors, to avoid imitating past styles and opt instead for a tasteful modern atmosphere is exemplified in the grand foyer. (Private Collection.)

But no artist contributed more to the Center's artistic panache than did Lee Lawrie. Born in Germany in 1877, Lawrie emigrated to the United States in the early 1890s, working first with sculptors in Chicago and later with Augustus Saint-Gaudens. His close collaboration with the architect Bertram Grosvenor Goodhue resulted in the awe-inspiring reredos at St. Thomas Church on Fifth Avenue, the magnificent figures on the west turrets of St. Vincent's Church on Lexington Avenue, and the four colossal symbolic statues flanking the main entrance of the Nebraska State Capitol in Lincoln. Lawrie, who died in 1963, was also the designer of the Franklin Delano Roosevelt dime. His oeuvre at Rockefeller Center included the vast images, 15 feet high and 55 feet wide, of *The Genius Who Interprets to the Human Race the Laws and Cycles of the Cosmic Figures of the Universe, Making the Cycles of Sight and Sound* on the principal façade of the

TOP Ladies' powder room with floral murals by Yasuo Kuniyochi. (Private Collection.)

BOTTOM Ruth Ceeves's cubistic *Jazz* patterned carpet for the grand foyer. (Private Collection.)

OPPOSITE Paul Manship's 1934 gilded bronze *Prometheus* in Rockefeller Center's lower plaza gets a polishing. (Photograph by Esther Bubley.)

RCA Building, the graceful intaglios above the north and south entrances of La Maison Française, the magnificent muscular bronze *Atlas* before the Fifth Avenue entrance to the International Building, and the composition above the International Building's 50th Street entrance.

Hood and Harrison's alma mater, the École des Beaux-Arts, taught that the first principle in effective urban planning was the axial plan: a street or boulevard or formal garden flanked by harmonious structures that leads to a clearly defined focal point. Thus pedestrians are drawn along the thoroughfare, animating the scene and contributing to the pleasure of city life. Paris is richly endowed with such aesthetic stratagems, preeminently the Champs Élysées moving majestically up to the Arc de Triomphe. The astute decision to place the comparatively low British Empire and La Maison Française buildings at Fifth Avenue on either side of the downward-sloping promenade—dubbed by journalists the Channel Gardens—leading to the upswept fin of the RCA Building, is classic Beaux Arts planning, Gotham's closest approximation to a Parisian boulevard.

When, on November 1, 1939, John D. Rockefeller, Jr., drove "the last rivet" to complete the steel skeleton of the U.S. Rubber Company Building, billed as the final structure of the center, he had reason to feel a satisfaction granted to few men. "They all laughed at Rockefeller Center," in the words of the Gershwin tune. Now they were indeed "fighting to get in." The critic Lewis Mumford, who had once sneered at the complex, was preparing to publish in the *New Yorker* his revised assessment that the center was "architecturally the most exciting mass of buildings in the city." In the course of the last rivet ceremony, Mayor Fiorello LaGuardia asked Rockefeller to create a few more such centers around the city. No wonder: the assessment on the structures in Rockefeller Center had jumped from zero in 1930 to almost 53$^1/_2$ million dollars in 1939.

Cover of *Showplace*, the Radio City Music Hall magazine, October 28, 1937, featuring the Music Hall's proscenium and the Rockettes. (Rockefeller Center Archives.)

Workers receiving their pay beside Rockefeller Center's first Christmas tree on Christmas Eve, 1931. (Private Collection.)

# THE 1939 FAIR: FAREWELL TO AN ERA

They are among New York's great lost treasures, ranking alongside Pennsylvania Station, the Singer Building, the Cornelius Vanderbilt mansion, and the Ziegfeld Theatre. They faultlessly expressed and emphatically concluded the Art Deco decades. Their very names, "Trylon" and "Perisphere," manifest that linguistic melding of science and popular culture so dear to the Deco heart. It was as though the precise word—"Plexiglas" or "neon" or "autogyro"—would whisk one away to an infinitely better world like that depicted in the 1936 film *Things to Come*, set in 2036 and based on an H. G. Wells novel. In that world, significantly, there was an infinite supply of golden, artificial sunlight.

ABOVE Hugh Ferriss's black and color crayon rendering of the Trylon and Perisphere under construction, 1938. (Avery Architectural and Fine Arts Library, Columbia University.)

OPPOSITE Visitors on the Helicline, the long, sloping, semicircular ramp by which they exited the Perisphere. (Thérèse Bonney/Bibliothèque Historique de la Ville de Paris.)

The Trylon, a triangular pylon 610 feet tall, was clearly visible, especially at night when it was lit, from as far away as the east side of Manhattan. Its sharp-edged geometric form harkened back to Cubism, to the early 20th-century paintings of Picasso and Braque, to the futuristic sets of films such as Fritz Lang's *Metropolis,* and to the stainless steel sky-piercing spire atop William Van Alen's Chrysler Building. Next to it, its companion in design, was the spheroid Perisphere, 180 feet in diameter. To support the enormous weight of the two structures—the Perisphere alone weighed 5,760 tons—their architects, the engineer J. André Fouilhoux and the designer Wallace K. Harrison, drove more than 1,000 pilings into the soggy fair site.

To enter the Perisphere, one rode up a 50-foot-high escalator—the tallest in the world—inside the Trylon and stepped out onto one of two moving rings located within a space twice the size of Radio City Music Hall. There viewers saw stretched out below them "Democracity," a lifelike diorama of a perfectly planned urban and suburban universe which vividly embodied the Fair's theme: "Building the World of Tomorrow."

The diorama was the centerpiece of a spectacular six-minute presentation which ended with the projection onto the ceiling of giant images of contented factory workers and happy farmers. The Perisphere wonderfully embodied the high quality invariably present in Art Deco design and display. Within a fabulous shell conceived by two architects who had been major players in the construction of Rockefeller Center, the diorama itself was the creation of Henry Dreyfuss, the man who had shaped the remarkable *Twentieth Century Limited.* The music accompanying the show, composed by William Grant Still, was conducted by Andre Kostelanetz, while the narration was by the noted newscaster H. V. Kaltenborn. Leaving the Perisphere, visitors descended the elegantly graceful Helicline, to which *Architectural Record* had given unqualified praise:

The pavilion for the renowned glassmaker Saint-Gobain by Rene Coulon and Jacques Adnet for the 1937 Paris Exposition. The exposition's modernistic architecture had a profound influence on that of the 1939 New York Fair. (Thérèse Bonney/Bibliotheque Historique de la Ville de Paris.)

Poster for the 1937 Paris Fair, color lithograph designed by Leonetto Cappiello. (Private Collection.)

"With its long line of people held confidently against the sky," the Helicline was "the finest element in the World's Fair."

One of the persistent criticisms of the Fair was its apparent neglect of religion. Indeed, after adverse comments about its absence from his Futurama in the General Motors Pavilion, Norman Bel Geddes added 600 churches to the display. But the criticism missed the obvious. The Trylon and the Perisphere were the basilica and campanile of America's secular faith in science in all its myriad applications from automobiles to airplanes, from ocean liners to radio, from phonograph records to motion pictures, from X-rays to refrigerators, from telephones to television. That was the belief which animated

317:—The Aviation Building

ABOVE The Aviation Building by William Lescaze and J. Gordon Carr was designed so that inside the pavilion visitors had the impression that they had arrived at a large, busy airport with airplanes in flight headed toward them. (Private Collection.)

the 1939 Fair, a very Art Deco belief. The form of the Perisphere expressed not only Art Deco's romance with geometry, but a conscious expression by Fouilhoux and Harrison of a tradition in sacred architecture which reached back to Rome's circular, domed Pantheon of the second century A.D. This tradition had been famously promulgated by the 16th-century Italian architect and theorist Andrea Palladio in his *The Four Books of Architecture*, where he asserted that for places of worship round was "the most beautiful." Palladio also set down the dictum that white was the only appropriate color for sacred buildings. It is therefore no accident that of the more than 300 structures at the 1939 Fair, the Trylon and the Perisphere were the only ones permitted to be painted pure white. The edifices in their immediate vicinity were painted off-white, while radiating from the Trylon and the Perisphere were avenues of gold, red, and blue with the tones darkening the further they moved from the Fair's radiant sacred center.

The Trylon and the Perisphere were almost universally admired. The *New York Times* wrote that they served their chief purpose well, which was to be the "great dominating structure to which the eye will be drawn, which will constantly orient the visitor, and which can serve as a symbol of the whole." Of all the international expositions which had followed in the wake of the first, that held in London in 1851, only New York in 1939 and the Paris Exposition of 1889, with its 984-foot-tall tower by Gustave Eiffel, had centerpieces which were immediately and universally recognized as "a symbol of the whole." Of the Eiffel Tower, the French writer Roland Barthes observed, "It became the symbol of Paris, of modernity, of communication, of science, of the nineteenth century." Substituting New York for Paris and twentieth for nineteenth century, one would have an apt description of the Trylon and Perisphere.

The 1939 Fair was an extraordinary act of faith. It was first bruited about in 1935 as a means of ameliorating New York City's desperate economic situation. Chicago's 1933 Century of Progress had cleared more than $500,000 and had been a bonanza for Windy City tourism. New York

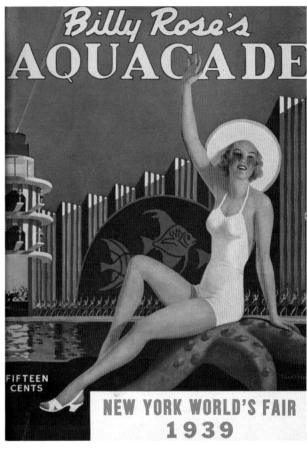

Billy Rose's Aquacade was the most successful presentation in the 280-acre amusement area. From its 12,000-seat amphitheater, designed by Sloan & Robertson, audiences were treated to spectacular shows staged by John Murray Anderson in its 275-foot-long pool. Among the Aquacade's stars were Johnny Weismuller, the current movie Tarzan, and Olympic champion Eleanor Holm. (Private Collection.)

OPPOSITE The Glass Building was one of the Fair's most spectacular nighttime sights. Designed by Shreve, Lamb, & Harmon, the architects of the Empire State Building, it was constructed almost entirely of plate glass and a favorite Art Deco building material, glass brick. Inside were exhibits by Corning Glass, promoting its Steuben Division; the Owens-Illinois Glass Company, featuring its line of Libbey tableware; and the Pittsburgh Plate Glass Company. (The Wurts Collection, Museum of the City of New York.)

ABOVE TOP The Transportation Zone was one of the Fair's most popular offerings. In the foreground is the Ford Motor Company's circular Road of Tomorrow on which visitors were given rides in new Fords, Mercurys, and Lincolns. The Ford Pavilion was by architect Albert Kahn with designer Walter Dorwin Teague. Beyond is the General Motors Pavilion, also by Kahn, with designer Norman Bel Geddes. In addition to automobiles, General Motors displayed Frigidaires and Diesel-electric locomotives. (Andre Vigneau/Bibliothèque de la Ville de Paris.)

ABOVE BOTTOM  Entry to Harrison & Fouilhoux's Electric Utilities exhibit was through a waterfall symbolizing hydroelectric power. The interior contrasted a street of 1892 with one of 1939 illustrating the good things which electricity had brought to America. (Avery Architectural and Fine Arts Library, Columbia University.)

hoped to do even better and it was certainly needed. It was estimated that out of a population of 7.5 million more than 1 million New Yorkers were unemployed. New Deal programs, such as the Works Progress Administration—the WPA—had put some 100,000 to work doing everything from improving parks to composing music, but the hard fact was that while such New Deal schemes provided temporary jobs and hope, the basic reality of persistent unemployment seemed intractable. In fact, only the advent of war production would solve it. Wits were not far from the truth when they gibed, "It is only the smooth dancing of Fred Astaire and the calming voice of F.D.R. which prevent the United States from having a revolution."

The moving forces behind the creation of the Fair were George McAneny, a banker who was head of the Regional Plan Association of New York, Percy Straus of Macy's, and Grover Whalen, a remarkable combination of magnetic charm and a fathomless capacity to make people cooperate. Whalen's resume was impressive. He had been New York's Police Commissioner and head of the IRT, and, as the city's official greeter, he had organized the ecstatic tickertape reception for Charles Lindbergh in 1927. Currently Whalen was president of Schenley distilleries. His enthusiasm for New York City was boundless. Typically, in the introduction to *New York: The World's Fair City*, published in 1937, he proclaimed: "It is the greatest city in the world; it is also the 'growingest' city in the world."

The Fair was incorporated in October 1935, with some one hundred leading New Yorkers as members. Almost immediately a group of architects, designers, and critics, including Walter Dorwin Teague, Harvey Wiley Corbett, and Lewis Mumford, organized an unofficial committee to take control of both the architectural aesthetics and the thematic direction of the Fair. Rejecting any Art Deco design, as embodied by the 1933 and 1937 Chicago and Paris expositions, the committee came down strongly on the side of what it saw as cutting-edge progressive architecture. This included both the International Style of the Bauhaus, as exemplified by the work of Mies van der Rohe, and the more romantic designs of Frank Lloyd Wright. There was also a clamor to abandon the idea of individual pavilions and substitute instead a single all-encompassing structure, a curious throwback to the 1851 London fair where some 100,000 exhibits had been housed in Joseph Paxton's immense iron and glass Crystal Palace. In addition, the committee urged the Fair to abandon the concept of "trade-show" commercialism and opt instead for a fair which would concentrate on educating the public as to the glorious prospect offered by a future in which every aspect of life was carefully planned. These proposals immediately encountered a hurricane of opposition from both the American Institute of Architects, who saw individual pavilions as a way to garner commissions for its members, and from prospective sponsors, who envisioned the fair as a mart in which to display and promote their wares and sniffed more than a whiff of anticapitalist, prosocialist bias in the proposals.

Hoping to calm the roiled waters, in 1936, the Fair Corporation made Grover Whalen its president. Whalen sought to soothe the ad-hoc committee by accepting as the theme of the Fair "Building the World of Tomorrow" and by splitting up the grounds into "zones" which included, in addition to obviously commercial ones like Transportation and Communications, others dedicated to public health and education. And in a move to both silence and subvert the committee, Whalen appointed his own seven-member board of design which included Stephen F. Voorhees, president of the American Institute of Architects; William Delano, a traditionalist architect of Georgian-style country residences and of opulent New York clubhouses like the Knickerbocker and the Union; and Gilmore D. Clarke, the distinguished landscape architect who had recently completed the highly praised Central Park Zoo. This board, deeply suspicious of both the aesthetics and the ideology of the radical architects, must be credited with bringing to the Fair a brilliant array of industrial designers with impeccable credentials: Donald Deskey, Russell Wright, Henry Dreyfuss, and Raymond Loewy. And with their power to reject or accept architects, the Board was, to a great degree, responsible for that galaxy of architects—James Gamble Rogers, Leonard Schultze, Philip Goodwin, Edward Durrell Stone, Ely Jacques Kahn, and others—who crafted the 1939 World's Fair's streamlined moderne style which was the final luminous flourish of American Art Deco.

If the Fair had an albatross around its neck, it was its remote location in the Borough of Queens, some eight miles from Times Square. The 1,216-acre site, bordering Flushing Bay, was a desolate marsh which for years had been the dumping ground for the waste from the Long Island Railroad's coal-burning locomotives. It had been famously described by F. Scott Fitzgerald in *The Great Gatsby* as "a valley of ashes." Robert Moses, who was, among other things, New York City's Parks Commissioner, proclaimed that the Fair was a chance to transform Flushing Meadows into another Central Park. The fact was that Moses had an obsession with highways, and his new extension of Grand Central Parkway, which hooked up with his new Triborough Bridge, linking Queens, Manhattan, and the Bronx, ran through Flushing's ash heaps. The Fair would funnel government funds to clear away the Long Island Railroad's mountains of clinkers. Its location in one of the "outer boroughs" deprived the Fair of the casual, drop-in visitor, the very type which had been a key element in the success of Chicago's Century of Progress, located on that city's lakefront, and of Paris's 1937 fair, sited along the Seine.

Midtown subway entrance displaying the Trylon and Perisphere. (Private Collection.)

ABOVE Century of Progress playing card by Joseph P. Birren. (Private Collection.)

RIGHT The modernistic architecture of Chicago's 1933 Century of Progress was a complete break from the Beaux Arts architecture of the Columbian Exposition held in the city in 1893. The tower rises from the Hall of Science in which the Century of Progress's central theme—applied science—was imaginatively presented. The hall's architect was Philadelphian Paul Cret. (Private Collection.)

While it is true a subway line had been extended to serve the Fair and the Long Island Railroad had built a special station there, getting to Flushing Meadows was no cinch. The 1939 *WPA Guide to New York City* sets forth the daunting details:

Transportation to the Fair, IRT subway to Times Square or Grand Central station, then by Flushing line; 23 minutes from Times Square; fare 5c. BMT Queens subway to Queens Plaza station, then by Flushing line; 26 minutes from Times Square; fare 5c. 8th Ave. (Independent) Queens subway (express) to Continental Ave. station, then by Queens crosstown line (local); 37 minutes from 42nd St., Manhattan; fare 10c. 2nd Ave. el (Flushing line); 30 minutes from 42nd St.; fare 5c. Long Island Railroad from Pennsylvania Station; 10 minutes; fare 10c on World's Fair trains only.

It is no wonder that Fair attendance never lived up to expectations. The Fair Corporation had predicted that 800,000 would come the first day. The figure was closer to 200,000. It had also predicted that attendance in 1939 would be 50 million. The actual figure was half that.

The memories of a six-year-old boy who attended the Fair are revealing:

We drove down to the City from Saratoga where my father had a stable of horses in training. When we got to the subway—I believe that it was Times Square—to go to the Fair, I was frightened. I had never been in a subway and the noise was terrific. It was summer, probably August, and it was hot in the subway car. Of course this was long before subway cars were air-conditioned. My father was wearing a coat and tie and a straw boater and I remember the perspiration pouring down his face. Everyone in the car was dressed up and they were all soaking wet. The ride took a long time.

Two things I vividly recall about the Fair were the huge figures projected onto the ceiling of the Perisphere. I loved movies—Shirley Temple was my goddess—and I thought this film projection truly wonderful. And in the entertainment section, there was a side show that was definitely not politically correct and one of the attractions was an armless man who could smoke by holding a cigarette between his toes. My father, who smoked cigars, was fascinated by that. When we got back to the City we went to a shop on the north side of 42nd Street near Fifth Avenue which sold American Indian things and my father bought me an Indian blanket for my bed. Coming out we looked up and there was the Empire State Building. I was reading "Jack and the Beanstalk" and it reminded me of the giant bean stalk in the book. Nothing at the Fair impressed me the way the Empire State Building did.*

Mayor Fiorello LaGuardia would have appreciated the encomium to the Empire State, for the day that the Fair opened, April 30, 1939, he had told the gathered throng: "May I point to one exhibit that I hope all visitors will note, and this is the City of New York itself."

Though the Fair opened on schedule and its organizers, at a cost of more than 160 million dollars, had built upon the slough of Flushing Meadows an alluring city, it was not without its critics. Those who had decried the Art Deco pavilions by Holabird & Root, Raymond Hood, and Paul Philippe Cret at Chicago in 1933 as "Buck Rogers Modernism" were quick to attack the Art Deco architecture of New York in 1939. "Architecturally the chief claim of the World's Fair on the attention of posterity will be the preposterous fact that Wright was not called to design it," Lewis Mumford snapped.

* From the memoir of David Garrard Lowe.

New York Parks Commissioner Robert Moses, left, Fair President Grover Whalen, center, and Mayor Fiorello LaGuardia huddle over plans for the 1939 Fair. (LaGuardia & Wagner Archives, LaGuardia Community College of the City of New York.)

The classical plan of the Fair was also decried as reactionary, looking to the past, not to the future. Indeed the streets radiating from the Trylon and Perisphere were strikingly reminiscent of Pierre L'Enfant's 18th-century plan for Washington, D.C., with the Fair's signature structures occupying the position of the U.S Capitol. The French magazine *L'Illustration* reported in its June 1939 issue, which featured the Fair, that there was a curious similarity between the layout of Paris's recent 1937 Exposition and that being held in New York. *L'Illustration* reinforced its argument by publishing the layouts of the two side by side.

The inescapable reality, though, was that the plan of the New York Fair worked magnificently on a practical level. It brought needed order to an enormous complex of 375 structures and made the visitor's task of planning sightseeing infinitely easier than had the individualistic layout of Chicago. The classical plan succeeded in Queens just as it did in Washington and in European cities where boulevards led to notable buildings and monuments. New York's layout not only emphasized the paramount position of the Trylon and Perisphere, but by means of the Fair's grandest esplanade which swept eastward to the Lagoon of Nations, visually linked them to James Earle Fraser's 65-foot-high statue of George Washington. This is one of the great, forgotten images of the Fair, the embodiment of the temporal reason for its being held in 1939 in New York. While Robert Moses made slighting comments about the anniversary, there is no doubt that federal funds for the project and the surprising participation of 33 states and territories were facilitated by the fact that the Fair marked the 150th anniversary of the first president's inauguration in New York City. The sculptor of the famed Indian-head nickel chose to portray Washington, not in the uniform of a soldier, but in civilian clothes of the type he might have worn for his swearing-in at Federal Hall on Nassau Street in 1789. At a time when armies were already clashing in Europe and in Asia, Fraser's gleaming white moderne statue inspired reassuring patriotism. A study of personal photograph albums of the Fair reveal that the most popular locale for snapshots was in front of the statue. At night, silhouetted against the flood-lit Perisphere, Washington became an American Zeus before his temple.

The pavilion which most perfectly melded the Fair's classic Deco style and the theme of the World of Tomorrow was that of General Motors. The largest pavilion—actually four connected structures—it was designed by the German-born Michigan architect, Albert Kahn. Kahn had a long history of working with Detroit's automotive giants, having created Ford's 2,000-acre River Rouge Plant in 1921 and the awesome General Motors Building in Detroit of 1922. The GM Pavilion's windowless main façade presented a high, suave cubistic curve which unfurled

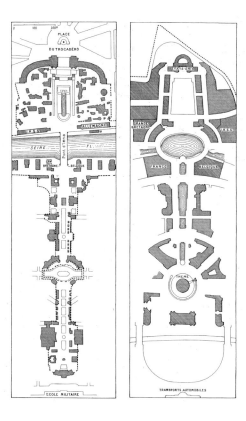

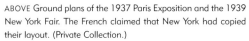

ABOVE Ground plans of the 1937 Paris Exposition and the 1939 New York Fair. The French claimed that New York had copied their layout. (Private Collection.)

RIGHT James Earle Frazier's huge statue of George Washington stood at one end of the Court of Peace, facing the Trylon and Perisphere and with its back to the Lagoon of Nations. (Private Collection.)

The railroad exhibit was sponsored by 28 different lines. The outdoor displays ranged from historic locomotives of the 1840s and 1850s to the glorious Art Deco 140-foot-long, 526-ton steam locomotive designed by Raymond Loewy for the Pennsylvania Railroad. (Private Collection.)

like a gigantic flag. Visitors entered the building through a tall groove cut into the façade to view the Fair's most sensational exhibit, Norman Bel Geddes's Futurama. Seated in one of the 600 chairs, they were taken by conveyor belt on a third-of-a-mile journey which simulated a cross-country airplane ride. Below was spread out Lippmann Geddes's startlingly realistic 35,000-square-foot model of America in 1960. It was an America where cities were concentrated into soaring 1,500-foot-tall towers while across the nation were scattered small towns in which agriculture, industry, and domesticity were in perfect balance. This being the pavilion of the manufacturer of Chevrolets, Pontiacs, Oldsmobiles, Buicks, Cadillacs, and La Salles, the America of 1960 was made possible, in no small part, by a stupendous highway system stretching from sea to sea over which automobiles raced at speeds of 100 miles per hour. In the two years that it was open, GM's Futurama attracted more than 25,000,000 visitors. Walter Lippmann, America's most respected pundit, saw a political and economic reality underlying this display sponsored by one of the nation's industrial powerhouses. Writing in the *New York Herald Tribune,* Lippmann observed: "This is what private enterprise can do, and the best that the Russians and the Italians have to show is no more than a feeble approximation of it."

It is significant that Lippmann should have mentioned the Soviet Union and Italy, for their pavilions were two of the most spectacular among those of the 60 nations and international

ABOVE Visitors viewing the Futurama display inside the General Motors Pavilion. More than 28,000 a day waited in line to see a model of America in 1960 which featured a landscape in which skyscrapers rose 1,500 feet into the air, an America without poverty or slums. (Fonds France Soir/Bibliothèque Historique de la Ville de Paris.)

LEFT The architecture of the United States Government Building, by Howard L. Cheney, mirrored the Art Deco classical federal structures, such as post offices and courthouses, being constructed across the country in the 1930s. The two towers were intended to symbolize the legislative and judicial branches of government, while the thirteen columns honored the original states. (Private Collection.)

TOP Among the most prominent of the foreign pavilions was that of the Union of Soviet Socialist Republics by Rois Iofan and Karo S. Alabian. Its tower was the tallest structure at the Fair after the Trylon. Among its exhibits was a replica of a sumptuous Moscow subway station. (Fonds France Soir/Bibliothèque Historique de la Ville de Paris.)

BOTTOM President Franklin Delano Roosevelt, Queen Elizabeth, the President's mother, Sara Delano Roosevelt, King George VI, and Eleanor Roosevelt at Hyde Park, June 11, 1939, the day after the royal couple visited the Fair. (Wide World Photos.)

organizations which participated in the Fair. The U.S.S.R. had been the first foreign government to sign up, and spent 6 million dollars on its building, a gargantuan horseshoe-shaped structure crowned by a tall tower faced with red Karlian marble—the same used for Lenin's tomb in Moscow—topped by a 79-foot-tall stainless steel statue of a worker which was quickly dubbed "Big Joe." The Soviet Union had had a similar pavilion in Paris in 1937, where it faced the vast German building designed by Albert Speer, whose soaring tower terminated in a fierce eagle with claws clutching a Nazi swastika. Germany had refused to exhibit in New York, giving as one of its reasons Mayor LaGuardia's outspoken opposition to Adolf Hitler's militarism and anti-Semitism.

A spectacular tower was also the chief design element of the Italian Pavilion, but this served as a plinth for *Roma*, an imposing seated figure with a waterfall tumbling at her feet. The hit of the Italian Pavilion was its second floor restaurant modeled on that of the Italian Line's opulent 1930s ocean liner, the *Conte di Savoia*. Its only gastronomic challenger was the restaurant in the French Pavilion, set amid displays of perfumes, cosmetics, and gowns by designers such as Jeanne Lanvin and Lucien Lelong. Faced with this plethora of pâté and pasta, the English wisely did not attempt to compete with the Italians or the French when it came to feeding fairgoers. They did have a popular tea room and a copy of the Magna Carta from Lincoln Cathedral. But the British had a sensational secret weapon, their new King George VI and his radiant Queen Elizabeth. The "Royal Visit" on Saturday, June 10, attracted hundreds of thousands of spectators and, at a crucial moment, helped immensely to nurture Anglo-American goodwill. The photographs of the King and Queen seated with President and Mrs. Roosevelt at Hyde Park the day after their visit to the Fair are undoubtedly among the most memorable images from the summer of 1939.

The initial season of the Fair ended on October 31, 1939. When it reopened in 1940 for its second and last season a number of changes were made in hopes of recouping the first year's 10-million-dollar operating deficit. Though Grover Whalen remained as the figurehead president, the man in charge was Harvey Dow Gibson of the Manufacturers Trust Company. To increase revenues, Gibson slashed admission from 75 to 50 cents, reduced rents to attract more exhibitors, and renamed the Amusement Area the "Great White Way," introducing more popular or, as some said, more vulgar, attractions.

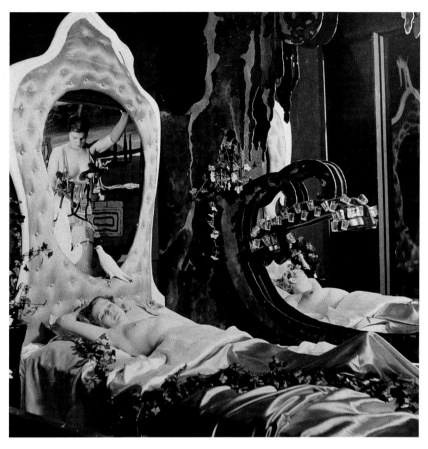

Undoubtedly the most sensational presentation at Flushing meadows was painter Salvador Dali's "Dream of Venus" pavilion. Conceived with the avant-garde New York gallery owner, Julien Levy, the pavilion was a surrealist celebration of female pulchritude. Its erotic tableaux, such as the "Bed of Venus," both shocked and titillated fairgoers. (Julien Levy/Bibliothèque Historic de la Ville de Paris.)

LEFT The Trylon and Perisphere instantly became worldwide symbols of the Fair and of New York. This jaunty advertisement appeared in the June 1939 issue of the French magazine, *L'Illustration*. (Private Collection.)

Poster for the 1939 World's Fair in New York. Color lithograph by Nembhard N. Culin. (Private Collection.)

In a world marching inexorably toward war, these changes at the Fair resembled nothing so much as the proverbial "rearranging deck chairs on the Titanic." Already in the summer of 1939, while New York newspapers reported such zippy happenings at Flushing Meadows as Boy Scouts' Day, the Belgian Pavilion's sparkling display of 20 million dollars worth of diamonds, and the election of Miss Nassau County, their pages were peppered with articles which resounded like sullen, distant thunder. These items were, in fact, the obituaries of an era: the Soviet premier reassured Poland that he saw relations improving; the Hamburg American liner, the *Saint Louis*, after being turned away from Havana and finding no port which would permit its passengers entry, carried its 917 German Jewish refugees back to Germany and almost certain death; Reich Marshall Hermann Goering welcomed home the Condor Legion which had fought alongside Franco in the Spanish Civil War; Premier Benito Mussolini greeted 20,000 Italian troops who had also fought for the Fascists in Spain and proclaimed they had a magnificent victory over "France, Great Britain, and the United States"; Chancellor Adolf Hitler told Prince Regent Paul of Yugoslavia that his nation's frontiers were "established for all time"; the Japanese continued their advance southward in China; 1,000 Czechs were arrested by armed Nazis in Bohemia-Moravia; President Roosevelt signed a bill appropriating funds for an enlarged American fleet, including two new 45,000-ton battleships.

By 1940 the impact of deteriorating world conditions on the Fair were inescapable. After being branded an aggressor for its attack on Finland, the Soviet Union packed up its pavilion and shipped it home, Argentina also departed, Norway and Denmark had a greatly reduced presence, and the British, under threat of imminent invasion, displayed a captured German parachute. By its last day, October 27, 1940 — eerily marked by a bugler sounding taps — German armies had pushed through Belgium and the Netherlands into France. On June 22, to the astonishment of the world and particularly to Americans, France surrendered. The Battle of Britain, with its attendant Blitz, had begun.

The Fair, like the sea retiring from the shore, left behind a number of surprising things. Unable to return to their homeland, the staff of the French Pavilion's restaurant opened in New York a sanctum sanctorum of *haute cuisine*, Le Pavilion; similarly, the chefs and waiters who had re-created the glories of the dining room of the *Conte di Savoia* in Flushing founded the Italian Pavilion in Manhattan. The heroic bronze statue of the Polish King Jagiello, who had defeated the Teutonic Knights in 1410, which had stood in front of Poland's Pavilion, found a peaceful home overlooking Turtle Pond in Central Park. There was a final, unambiguous signal that the Art Deco world, which had believed science benign and technology the compassionate guide to a progressively better universe, had expired. The very sphere, the Perisphere, which had gaily celebrated The World of Tomorrow with its Democracity, was, after the Fair ended, demolished. Its 4,000 tons of steel were converted into weapons of war, thus reversing the prophesy of Micah that "they shall beat their swords into plowshares, and their spears into pruning hooks."

Abbot, Willis J. *The United States in the Great War*, Leslie-Judge, New York, 1919.

Adler, Dennis. *Mercedes-Benz: 110 Years of Excellence*, MBI Publishing, Osceola, Wisconsin, 1995.

Albrecht, Donald. *Designing Dreams: Modern Architecture in the Movies*, Hennessey & Ingalls, Santa Monica, Calif., 2000.

Allen, Frederick Lewis. *The Big Change*, Harper & Brothers, New York, 1952.

Alpern, Andrew. *The New York Apartment Houses of Rosario Candela and James Carpenter*, Acanthus, New York, 2001.

Amory, Cleveland, and Frederic Bradlee, (eds.). *Vanity Fair: Selections from America's Most Memorable Magazine*, Viking, New York, 1960.

Amory, Cleveland. *Who Killed Society?* Harper & Brothers, New York, 1960.

Andrist, Ralph K., and Edmund Stillman. *The American Heritage History of the 20s and 30s*, American Heritage, New York, 1970.

Arwas, Victor. *Art Deco*, Abrams, New York, 1992.

Atkinson, Brooks. *Broadway*, Macmillan, New York, 1970.

Battersby, Martin. *The Decorative Thirties* (revised and edited by Philippe Garner), Watson-Guptill, New York, 1988.

Battersby, Martin. *The Decorative Twenties*, Walker, New York, 1969.

Bayer, Patricia. *Art Deco: Design, Decoration and Detail from the Twenties and Thirties*, Thames & Hudson, London, 1992.

Beaton, Cecil Walter Hardy. *Cecil Beaton's New York*, Lippincott, Philadelphia, 1938.

Beebe, Lucius Morris. *Snoot If You Must*, Appleton-Century, New York, 1943.

Bel Geddes, Norman. *Horizons*, Little, Brown, Boston, 1932.

Bollack, Françoise, and Tom Killian. *Ely Jacques Kahn: New York Architect*, Acanthus, New York, 1995.

Bragdon, Claude. *The Frozen Fountain: Being Essays on Architecture and the Art of Design in Space*, Knopf, New York, 1932.

Braynard, Frank O. *Picture History of the Normandie*, Dover, New York, 1987.

Brinnin, John Malcolm, and Kenneth Gaulin. *Grand Luxe: The Transatlantic Style*, Henry Holt, New York, 1988.

Brinnin, John Malcolm. *The Sway of the Grand Saloon: A Social History of the North Atlantic*, Delacorte, New York, 1971.

Brunhammer, Yvonne. *The Art Deco Style*, St. Martin's, New York, 1984.

Carter, Randolph and Robert Reed Cole. *Joseph Urban: Architecture, Theatre, Opera, Film*, Abbeville, New York, 1992.

Carter, Randolph, and Robert Reed Cole. *Joseph Urban*, Abbeville, New York, 1992.

Chamberlain, Samuel (ed.). *Rockefeller Center: A Photographic Narrative*, Hastings House, New York, 1937.

Cohen, Barbara, Seymour Chwast and Steven Heller (eds.). *New York Observed: Artists and Writers Look at the City*, Abrams, New York, 1987.

Cumming, Elizabeth, and Wendy Kaplan. *The Arts and Crafts Movement*, Thames & Hudson, London, 1991.

de Chambrun, Clara Longworth. *Shadows Lengthen: The Story of My Life*, Scribner's, New York, 1949.

Deshoulières, Dominique, and Hubert Jeanneau, (eds.). *Rob Mallet-Stevens: Architecte*, Editions, Archives d'Architecture Moderne, Bruxelles, 1980.

Drennan, Robert E. (ed.). *The Algonquin Wits*, Citadel Press, New York, 1968.

Duncan, Alastair (ed.). *The Encyclopedia of Art Deco*, Dutton, New York, 1988.

Ellis, Edward Robb. *A Nation in Torment: The Great American Depression*, Capricorn, New York, 1971.

Farrell, Frank. *The Greatest of Them All*, Giniger, New York, 1982.

Fitch, James Marston. *American Building*, Schocken, New York, 1973.

Fitzgerald, F. Scott. *Babylon Revisited and other Stories*, Scribner's, New York, 1971.

Fitzgerald, F. Scott. *Tender Is the Night*, Scribner's, New York, 1933.

Flinchum, Russell. *Henry Dreyfuss, Industrial Designer*, Rizzoli, New York, 1997.

Galante, Pierre. *Mademoiselle Chanel,* Henry Regnery, Chicago, 1973.

Gallo, Max. *The Poster in History,* with essays by Carlo Arturo Quintavalle and Charles Flowers, W. W. Norton, New York, 2000.

Gill, Brendan. *Happy Times,* with photographs by Jerome Zerbe, Harcourt Brace Jovanovich, New York, 1973.

Goldstone, Harman H., and Martha Dalrymple. *History Preserved; A Guide to New York City Landmarks and Historic Districts,* Simon & Schuster, New York, 1974.

Gosling, Nigel. *The Adventurous World of Paris 1900–1914,* Morrow, New York, 1978.

Haedrich, Marcel. *Coco Chanel: Her Life, Her Secrets,* Little, Brown, Boston, 1972.

Hemingway, Ernest. *The Sun Also Rises,* Scribner's, New York, 1926.

Heppenheimer, T. A. *A Brief History of Flight: From Balloons to Mach 3 and Beyond,* Wiley, New York, 2001.

Howard, Michael. *The First World War,* Oxford Univ. Press, New York, s2002.

Johnson, Philip C. *Mies Van Der Rohe,* Museum of Modern Art, distributed by New York Graphic Society, 1978.

Johnston, Bob, and Joe Welsh with Mike Schafer. *The Art of the Streamliner,* MetroBooks, New York, 2001.

Josephy, Helen, and Mary Margaret McBride. *New York Is Everybody's Town,* Putnam, New York, 1931.

*Otto Wagner.* Janos Kalmar (photographer), TeNeues, Dusseldorf, 2002.

Keats, John. *You Might As Well Live: The Life and Times of Dorothy Parker,* Simon & Schuster, New York, 1970.

Kert, Bernice. *Abby Aldrich Rockefeller: The Woman in the Family,* Random House, New York, 1993.

Kimball, Robert (ed.). *Cole: A Biographical Essay by Brendan Gill,* Holt, Rinehart, New York, 1971.

Krinsky, Carol Herselle. *Rockefeller Center,* Oxford Univ. Press, New York, 1978.

Laver, James. *Costume and Fashion: A Concise History,* Thames & Hudson, New York, 2002.

Lent, Henry B. *The Waldorf-Astoria,* Hotel Waldorf-Astoria, 1934.

Loewy, Raymond. *Never Leave Well Enough Alone,* Simon & Schuster, New York, 1951.

Longford, Elizabeth. *The Queen Mother, Elizabeth: Consort of George VI,* William Morrow, New York, 1981.

Loos, Anita. *A Girl Like I,* Viking, New York, 1966.

Lottman, Herbert R. *Man Ray's Montparnasse,* Abrams, New York, 2001.

Lowe, David Garrard. Beaux Arts New York, Watson-Guptill, New York, 1988.

Lowe, David Garrard. *Lost Chicago* (rev. ed.), Watson-Guptill, New York, 2000.

Lynn, Kenneth S. *Hemingway,* Simon & Schuster, New York, 1987.

Lyons, Eugene. *David Sarnoff,* Harper & Row, New York, 1966.

Manchester, William. *Disturber of the Peace: The Life of H. L. Mencken,* Univ. of Massachusetts Press, Amherst, 1986.

Mandelbaum, Howard, and Eric Myers. *Screen Deco,* St. Martin's Press, New York, 1985.

Martin, Hervé. *Guide de L'Architecture Moderne à Paris,* Editions Alternatives, Paris, 1986.

McBrien, William. *Cole Porter: A Biography,* Knopf, New York, 1998.

Meade, Marion. *Dorothy Parker: What Fresh Hell Is This?,* Villard, New York, 1989.

Mellow, James R. *Hemingway: A Life Without Consequences,* Houghton Mifflin, Boston, 1992.

Meyers, Jeffrey. *Hemingway: A Biography,* Harper & Row, New York, 1985.

Middlemas, Keith. *The Life and Times of George VI,* Weidenfeld & Nicolson, London, 1974.

Morris, Sylvia Jukes. *Rage for Fame: The Ascent of Clare Boothe Luce,* Random House, New York, 1997.

Newhouse, Victoria. *Wallace K. Harrison, Architect,* Rizzoli, New York, 1989.

Olian, Joanne (ed.). *Authentic French Fashions of the Twenties,* New York, Dover, 1990.

Oliver, Richard. *Bertram Grosvenor Goodhue,* Architectural History Foundation, New York, MIT Press, Cambridge, Mass., 1983.

Packer, William. *Fashion Drawings in Vogue,* Coward-McCann, New York, 1983.

*The Park Avenue Cubists: Gallatin, Morris, Frelinghuysen and Shaw,* with essays by Debra Bricker Balken and Robert S. Lubar. Grey Art Gallery, New York University, 2003.

Parker, Dorothy. *Constant Reader,* Viking, New York, 1970.

Parker, Dorothy. *Stories, Wings,* Random House, New York, 1992.

Pevsner, Nikolaus. *Pioneers of Modern Design: From William Morris to Walter Gropius,* Penguin, Hammondsworth, U.K., 1991.

Pinchon, Jean-François (ed.). *Robert Mallet-Stevens: Architecture, Furniture, Interior Design,* MIT Press, Cambridge, Mass., 1990.

Post, Edwin. *Truly Emily Post,* Funk & Wagnalls, New York, 1961.

Reier, Sharon. *The Bridges of New York,* Dover, New York, 1977.

Robinson, Cervin, and Rosemarie Haag Bletter. *Skyscraper Style: Art Deco New York,* Oxford Univ. Press, New York, 1975.

*Rockefeller New York: A Tour by Henry Hope Reed.* Photographs by Esther Bubley, Greensward Foundation, New York, 1988.

Rogers, Agnes, and Frederick Lewis Allen. *I Remember Distinctly: A Family Album of the American People 1918–1914,* Harper and Brothers, New York, 1947.

Ross, Josephine. *Society in Vogue: The International Set between the Wars,* Vendome, New York, 1992.

Schorske, Carl E. *Fin-de-Siècle Vienna: Politics and Culture,* Vintage, New York, 1981.

Sears, Stephen W. *The American Heritage History of the Automobile in America,* American Heritage, New York, 1977.

Slavin, Richard E. III. *Opulent Textiles: The Schumacher Collection,* Crown, New York, 1992.

Snow, Carmel, with Mary Louise Aswell. *The World of Carmel Snow,* McGraw-Hill, New York, 1962.

Stern, Robert A. M., Gregory Gilmartin, and Thomas Mellins. *New York 1930: Architecture and Urbanism between the Two World Wars,* Rizzoli, 1987.

Sussman, Elisabeth, with John G. Hanhardt. *City of Ambition: Artists & New York 1900–1960,* Whitney Museum of American Art, New York, in association with Flammarion, Paris, 1996.

Thomas, Bernice L. *America's 5 & 10 Cent Stores: The Kress Legacy,* National Building Museum Preservation Press, Wiley, New York, 1997.

Tunick, Susan. *Terra-Cotta Skyline: New York's Architectural Ornament,* Princeton Architectural Press, New York, 1997.

Van de Lemme, Arie. *A Guide to Art Deco Style,* Chartwell, 1986.

Waggoner, Susan. *Nightclub Nights: Art, Legend and Style 1920–1960,* Rizzoli, New York, 2001.

Walker, Stanley. *The Night Club Era,* Johns Hopkins Univ. Press, Baltimore, 1933.

Wallach, Janet. *Chanel: Her Style and Her Life,* N. Talese, New York, 1998.

Weber, Eva. *Art Deco in North Ammerica,* Bison Books, London, 1985.

West, Charlotte C. *Ageless Youth,* Crowell, New York, 1929.

*The WPA Guide to New York City: The Federal Writers' Project Guide to 1930s New York.* Introduction by William H. Whyte, New Press, New York, 1995.

Yoxall, H. W. *A Fashion of Life,* Heinemann, London and New York, 1966.

Zaczek, Iain. *Essential Art Deco,* Paragon House, Bath, U.K., 2000.